SANDETTIE LIGHT

by the same author

poetry
ZOOM!
XANADU
KID
BOOK OF MATCHES
THE DEAD SEA POEMS
MOON COUNTRY
(with Glyn Maxwell)
CLOUDCUCKOOLAND
KILLING TIME
SELECTED POEMS
TRAVELLING SONGS
THE UNIVERSAL HOME DOCTOR
TYRANNOSAURUS REX VERSUS THE CORDUROY KID
OUT OF THE BLUE
SEEING STARS
PAPER AEROPLANE
(Selected Poems 1989–2014)
STILL
THE UNACCOMPANIED
MAGNETIC FIELD

drama
ECLIPSE
MISTER HERACLES
(after Euripides)
JERUSALEM
HOMER'S ODYSSEY
THE LAST DAYS OF TROY
THE ODYSSEY: MISSING PRESUMED DEAD

prose
ALL POINTS NORTH
LITTLE GREEN MAN
THE WHITE STUFF
GIG
WALKING HOME
WALKING AWAY

translation
SIR GAWAIN AND THE GREEN KNIGHT
THE DEATH OF KING ARTHUR
PEARL

SIMON ARMITAGE

Sandettie Light Vessel Automatic

FABER & FABER

First published in 2019
by Faber & Faber Ltd
Bloomsbury House
74–77 Great Russell Street
London WC1B 3DA
This paperback edition first published in 2020

Typeset by Donald Sommerville
Printed in the UK by TJ International Ltd, Padstow, Cornwall

A CIP record for this book is available from the British Library

ISBN 978-0-571-33497-1

FSC
www.fsc.org
MIX
Paper from
responsible sources
FSC® C013056

10 9 8 7 6 5 4 3 2 1

Contents

[vii]

Acknowledgements

Where not specifically mentioned in the Notes, acknowledgements are due to the following:

Academy of American Poets, *Australian Book Review*, *Cordite Poetry Review*, *Daily Telegraph*, Durham Literature Festival, Free Verse: The Poetry Book Fair, *Guardian*, The Lives of Houses (Oxford Centre for Life-Writing), *New Statesman*, *Observer*, *Oxford Review of Books*, *Plume*, *PN Review*, *Poetry and Audience*, Poetry Archive, Poetry Foundation, *Sewanee Review*.

Introduction

Ever since my earliest encounters with poetry I always believed it had the persuasive power to operate beyond the printed page and away from traditional literary environments. If I could hear poetic phrases in speeches, songs and everyday conversations, and witness poetic techniques at work (often perniciously) on advertising billboards, in newspaper headlines and within the wider media, what was to stop *actual poems* functioning and flourishing in unusual or unexpected locations – within radio and television documentaries, on posters, at concerts, on the side of a building or the face of a quarry in the middle of a moor, and in many other non-literary spaces. In fact there's an argument to say that poetry is at its most effective when it appears without warning and outside its own comfort zones. *Poetry on the Underground* demonstrated as much, before it became a familiar element of Tube transport in the capital, alongside adverts for multivitamins and hair transplants. Looking back, Philip Larkin's late poem 'Bridge for the Living' provided a useful benchmark. Conceived as a 'lyric' for a musical cantata (by the composer Anthony Hedges) to celebrate the opening of the Humber Bridge, its last line, 'Always it is by bridges that we live' is an unusually optimistic conclusion for a poet more given to exploring societal separation and interpersonal disconnection. Yet the trademark sighs and frowns and the incisive observational descriptions are all there, Larkin pulling off a seemingly unenviable task without the kind of cringing and blushing we expect when high-minded literature is unveiled to the glare of the everyday and when reluctant poets are paraded in front of unaccustomed audiences.

Poetry need not be an autonomous or hermetically sealed activity, as its long-established relationship with theatre and drama makes clear. To that end, I have always been keen to collaborate with other artists and also with individuals and organisations away from the creative industries, and this anthology is a selected portfolio of the resulting work. Some of the poems have been published before, though never as part of a dedicated volume, and others are making their debuts for the first time within the supporting context of poems conceived in the same spirit. Not everything has been included – it would have made the volume impractically large. Omissions include a substantial number of poems and song lyrics written for film, radio and stage which are generally available elsewhere, and poems that have found a settled existence in other formats, and one or two pieces written ostensibly for the voice which rejected my attempts to wrangle them into a typographic arrangement. It is also the case that two or three of the poems have been somewhat migratory, starting out in one place (e.g. as a chorus in a re-dramatised Greek play) and ending up somewhere else (e.g. as the lyrics for a track on a spoken-word album). It would be easy enough to admit that such 'repurposing' makes the poems (or perhaps more accurately the poet) mercenary in nature, but packages of script aren't always conceived within or delivered into the most advantageous situations, and sometimes find more success elsewhere. Edward Thomas's 'Adlestrop' was originally a prose entry in his journal. Since Horace first composed the line 'Dulce et decorum est pro patria mori' it has served all kinds of purposes, but never more powerfully than in Wilfred Owen's famous poem, deployed to both ironic and tragic effect. And Christina Rossetti's 'In the Bleak Midwinter' is a better carol than a poem – far more poignant and tender – especially when sung to Holst's 'Cranham' setting.

Extensive notes follow the poems as a way of providing background information on the projects, in case an appreciation of the original assignment is necessary for a sympathetic reading of the work. I'd like to thank the great number of people involved in these commissions for their invitations, their cooperation, their trust, and on some occasions their patience. All these endeavours allowed me to step away from the conventional practice of producing a 'full-length collection' every three or four years to pursue a different kind of writing – one that views poetry as a *trade* (in both the noun and the verb sense) and as a *craft*, with its implication of form and function. Like the craft of this book's title, perhaps, fulfilling a practical service as a navigational device in the English Channel while offering imaginative possibilities as part of the hypnotic litany of the Maritime and Coastguard Agency's Shipping Forecast.

SIMON ARMITAGE
2019

[xv]

SANDETTIE LIGHT VESSEL AUTOMATIC

Sulpicia's Playlist

'Uh-oh, Love Comes To Town'
from the 77 album by Talking Heads.
'Let Them All Talk' by Elvis Costello,
from *Punch the Clock*, reissued on digital cassette.

'How Spook Got Her Man' by Felt,
from *The Pictorial Jackson Review* LP.
'Rape Me' by Nirvana,
from *In Utero*, on CD.

'Bigmouth Strikes Again' by The Smiths,
on the Rough Trade label.
'Rip It Up' by Orange Juice;
the picture disc single.

'I Can't Help Myself' by Orange Juice,
from *Rip It Up*, the album.
'The Final Resting of the Ark' by Felt,
on vinyl.

Making a Name

Here is a name – it is your name for life.
Loop it around your ears and toes – it works
like puppet strings, like radio control.
Try it for sound – slide it between your teeth.

Stitch that name into your socks and vest.
Sketch the shape of your name with a felt tip.
Will it float or fly, or should it be screwed
to an office door, propped on a desk?

Once we were named by our quirks and kinks,
known by our lazy eyes, our harelips.
Once we were named by the knack of our hands:
we were fletchers, bakers, coopers, smiths.

Don't sell your name to a man in a bar!
Don't leave your name in a purse on the beach!
Don't wait for a blue plaque – get yourself known
with glitter and glue, in wrought iron-work;

sign your autograph with a laser-pen
on the face of the moon. Here is your name
and a lifetime only to make it your own.
Then the mason takes it, sets it in stone.

The Not Dead

We are the not dead.
In battle, life would not say goodbye to us.
And crack shot snipers seemed to turn a blind eye to us.
And even though guns and grenades let fly at us
we somehow survived.

We are the not dead.
When we were young and fully alive for her,
we worshipped Britannia.
We the undersigned
put our names on the line for her.
From the day we were born we were loaded and
primed for her.
Prepared as we were, though, to lie down and die for her,
we somehow survived.

So why did she cheat on us?
Didn't we come running when she most needed us?
When tub-thumping preachers
and bullet-brained leaders
gave solemn oaths and stirring speeches
then fisted the air and pointed eastwards,
didn't we turn our backs on our nearest and dearest?
From runways and slipways Britannia cheered us,
but returning home refused to meet us,
sent out a crowd of back-biting jeerers

and mealy-mouth sneerers.
Two-timing, two-faced Britannia deceived us.

We are morbidly ill.
Soldiers with nothing but time to kill,
we idle now in everyday clothes and ordinary towns,
blowing up, breaking down.
If we dive for cover or wake in a heap,
Britannia, from horseback, now crosses the street
or looks right through us.
We seem changed and ghostly to those who knew us.
The country which flew the red white and blue for us
now shows her true colours.
We are the not dead.
Neither happy and proud
with a barcode of medals across the heart
nor laid in a box and draped in a flag,
we wander this no man's land instead,
creatures of a different stripe – the awkward, unwanted,
unlovable type –
haunted with fear and guilt,
wounded in spirit and mind.

So what shall we do with the not dead and all of his kind?

The Black Swans

Through a panel of glass in the back of the wagon
the country went past. You clean your weapon,
make camp, drive around, stand guard, stand down.
Sit with a gun in your hand and your thumb up your arse.
Or you try to get shot at – just for a laugh.

Nineteen, fighting the boredom, wearing a blue lid.
Then one day the kid who gets smokes for the lads
walks into the woods and never comes back.
Then one day the Black Swans drive by in a van –
a death squad of Bennies in bobble hats,
wielding Kalashnikovs,
smirking, running their fingers across their throats.
Not to be checked or blocked. A law unto themselves.

Walk in the valley. Walk in the shadow of death
in the wake of the Black Swans, treading the scorched earth.
Houses trashed and torched. In a back yard
a cloud of bluebottles hides a beheaded dog.
This woman won't talk, standing there open-mouthed,
tied to a tree, sliced from north to south.
In the town square, a million black-eyed bullet holes stare
and stare. Crows lift from the mosque. Behind the school,
flesh-smoke – sweet as incense – rises and hangs
over mounds of soil planted with feet and hands.

Albion

I was a boy soldier, back when grenades were pine cones
and guns were sticks.

I played Churchill's speeches, fought on the beaches
as Vera Lynn
sang from the white cliffs,

and I dreamed the dream of a hero's welcome,
of flags and bunting
lining the streets,

of drinking for free in every bar, of beautiful women
with open arms
and white cotton sheets.

But instead of klaxons and Union Jacks came sticking plasters
to cover the cracks,

and ibuprofen to ease the mind. Without blood or scars
or a missing leg
you're swinging the lead;

without entry wounds and exit wounds or burns to the face
you're just soft in the head,

and the British Army isn't the place for a lying bastard
or basket case.

What I did, I did for St George and for England and God;
now I sleep in sweat,

slaying the dragon or training the crosshairs
on mum and dad
and shooting them dead.

Distraction helps. The beast stalks in the day,
kept back by the noise
and the light,

but after the action, emptiness falls on the Hawthorns
and darkness stirs.
Then cometh the night.

Remains

On another occasion, we get sent out
to tackle looters raiding a bank.
And one of them legs it up the road,
probably armed, possibly not.

Well myself and somebody else and somebody else
are all of the same mind,
so all three of us open fire.
Three of a kind all letting fly, and I swear

I see every round as it rips through his life –
I see broad daylight on the other side.
So we've hit this looter a dozen times
and he's there on the ground, sort of inside out,

pain itself, the image of agony.
One of my mates goes by
and tosses his guts back into his body.
Then he's carted off in the back of a lorry.

End of story, except not really.
His blood-shadow stays on the street, and out on patrol
I walk right over it week after week.
Then I'm home on leave, but I blink

and he bursts again through the doors of the bank.
Sleep, and he's probably armed, possibly not.
Dream, and he's torn apart by a dozen rounds.
And the drink and the drugs won't flush him out –

he's here in my head when I close my eyes,
dug in behind enemy lines,
not left for dead in some distant, sun-fucked,
stone age land
or six-feet-under in desert sand,

but near to the knuckle, here and now,
his bloody life in my bloody hands.

Warriors

It's just one massive ditch, the border with Kuwait,
and once over the bun-line the heart bounces and kicks,
expecting fury unleashed, the mother of all fights,
a million madmen in sandals all armed to the teeth.
But there's only sand and some goat-boy walking his herd.
The gun-turret spins a full 360 degrees – like an owl's head.

Rumble onward all night till you're just about cooked.
The section commander gets out for a piss and almost
            loses his cock.
Crunch over something brittle, plough through
            something soft,
rounds pinging the metal like jet-propelled wasps,
the Warrior slewing and spinning. It roars forward, then stops.
Range 410 miles, road speed 46 miles per hour – tops.

Banged up for nine hours in half-light and slow heat,
but it's only the last thirty seconds that truly count,
before the lid comes off. As the last moments are dealt out
some guys scream and shout, bringing their blood to the boil;
others stare into friends' eyes, right to the back of the skull.
Deployment is via a hydraulic door in the hull.

What happens thereafter, either I won't say, or can't.
To survive, good infantrymen keep their emotions locked
and imaginations screwed shut. If not, the door of the truck
becomes like the back of an old-fashioned camera: open it up
and the sun floods in, blazes the film, and you're fucked.
A Rolls Royce V8 Condor engine grinds sand in its guts.

Scarecrows

Life wants to live, and nature will lift and restore
the fallen and broken.
Nevertheless, a hose-pipe snakes through the vehicle door,
and you sit there, son, with the engine purring,
not to be woken,
breathing the fumes till the world stops turning.

They'll be harvesting now in parts of the Balkans,
carts piled high,
patches of earth unpredictably fertile. Fruitful.
From blister-packs and childproof bottles
you count out the pills,
swilling them down with vodka and Red Bull.

In the butcher's window, a side of beef
is precisely a corpse.
A slash to the wrists would be painless and quick
if the blade was keen and the hand held steady,
but you flinch from the thought,
having witnessed so much of your blood already.

The trees are waiting, heaven-sent. Sling a rope
from a lime or an oak –
(how good does it feel, the noose on the throat?) –
and swing from a branch, but the branch won't hold.
Then wake in sweat
with your hands in a knot around Laura's neck.

A birthday balloon goes off like a bomb
and a car backfires.

But you, you're a son of the soil, are you not?
So take up your gun
and shoot yourself stupid, blank after blank,
over and over again till the hands don't shake,
and the nerves don't *feel*,
and the crows have risen and flapped
from the ploughed field.

The Malaya Emergency

One road in, one road out.
A world away from a bricklayer's yard,
from Manchester's oily ship canal
to a tented camp on a river bank.
River runs deep. River runs dark.

One road there, one road back.
Leaf-light dapples a mountain track.
Then all-out attack.
Buds like bullets, flowers like flack.
River runs thick, river runs fast.

Me and Lomas and Polish John.
We sat and thought.
Whispered and smoked.
Men without rank, men on their own.
One road out, one road home . . .

so we drove back into the killing zone,
just drove right into the killing zone,

river still rolling, turning its stones,
mates I'd drank and laughed and joked with,
mates I'd effed and jeffed and smoked with
are butchered now and their shirts are burning,
river still writhing, river still turning,
Joe with his eye shot out of his head,
(he'll live for now but meet his end
in a Manchester doorway, begging for bread),
river runs black, river runs red,
some boy wailing his mother's name,
Tommy asleep with a hole in his brain . . .
I found his killer and shot him dead,
tossed him onto a barbed wire fence,
taught him a lesson, left him to rot.

Job done.
Till thirty years on,
when the dead, like the drowned, float up to the top.

One road out, one road in.
And all for what – rubber and tin.
A can of beans, a bicycle tyre.
A river in flames, a river on fire.
A bicycle tyre and a can of beans
and a river that streams and streams and streams.

The Parting Shot

So five graves, like long evening shadows, are dug,
and the five coffins wait in line, varnished
and squared off,
and the firing party aims for the distance and fires,
and all are starched and suited and booted
and buttoned up.

Then ramrod straight, under the shade of a tree,
the boy-bugler raises a golden horn to his lips,
and calls to his dead friends with his living breath.
And the tune never wavers or breaks,
but now tears roll from his eyes,
tears which fall from his face and bloom
on his ironed green shirt like two dark wounds.

Then the world swims and drowns
in everyone else's eyes too.

The Manhunt

After the first phase,
after passionate nights and intimate days,

only then would he let me trace
the frozen river which ran through his face,

only then would he let me explore
the blown hinge of his lower jaw,

and handle and hold
the damaged, porcelain collar-bone,

and mind and attend
the fractured rudder of shoulder-blade,

and finger and thumb
the parachute silk of his punctured lung.

Only then could I bind the struts
and climb the rungs of his broken ribs,

and feel the hurt
of his grazed heart.

Skirting along,
only then could I picture the scan,

the foetus of metal beneath his chest
where the bullet had finally come to rest.

Then I widened the search,
traced the scarring back to its source

to a sweating, unexploded mine
buried deep in his mind, around which

every nerve in his body had tightened and closed.
Then, and only then, did I come close.

PETER AND THE WOLF

Cat

The wind in the grass
will come to pass,
and the wind in the trees
is only a breeze,
and the wind in the leaves
for all that it sighs
and all that it heaves
is only the leaves.
But the wind in the reed
as it lives and breathes,
as it preens and purrs,
comes slinking forward
with claws for fingers
and draped in furs.

Grandfather

Where the old boy goes
he shuffles and slows,
and sometimes sinks
to his pillows and sheets
to inspect his eyelids,
for forty winks.

And whenever he sleeps
he snores and snores,
and up from the bed
like a swarm of Zeds
comes a long slow croon,
comes a low-slung drone,
a snoozy, syrupy, boozy tune.
You poor old soul.
You old bassoon.

Duck

You're all neck,
made to dabble and peck,
with a sticky-out reed
that's nothing less
than a bill or a beak,
grubbing and scraping
for crumbs and weeds.
Then open your mouth,
and a tune bubbles out
that quavers and soothes
and waddles and slews
from leg to leg
and rolls like an egg,
the kind of thing
that a duck might sing,
if a duck had a song.

But you're no swan.

Bird

Oh small thin flute
in your long silver coat,
with your sixpence buttons
like moon-coloured medals,
and your tight little throat
and twittering, fluttering, tip-toeing notes.
Oh small thin flute,
once you've been heard
you're no flute:
you're a bird.

Hunters

You campfire swearers,
you rabbit snarers,
you moleskin wearers,
you vixen skinners,
you marrow diggers,
you trackers and trailers,
you scalpers and scalers,
you hiders and skulkers,
you skull-busting hunters,
you pair of chumps
in your clomping boots,
you galumphing shooters,
you rifling looters,
you blunderbuss thugs,

you thundering fools,
you blundering chums,

you pair of proper kettle drums.

Peter

Little kid, all buttoned up,
all tied at the tongue
and sewn at the lips,
all wordless and schtum
with your jacket zipped
to right under your chin . . .
And you're so thin,
as wiry and thin
as a length of string,
as lean and as taut
as catgut or steel,
a living, walking violin,
so the faintest brush
with nothing more
than a horse's hair
and we hear what you feel.
We can see your soul.

Wolf

Quicksilver dog,
worst kind of cross
between bear and fox,
one ghosts between trees,
or the whole pack flows
like the wind or a stream.
Dog of hell-frozen-over,
wherever you run
the end of the world
must also come.
Apparition. Silhouette.
Mist-hound,
moon-hound,
dog with the eyes
of arctic ice,
on the ridge on your own,
snuffing out light
with a snarl or a scowl,
summoning night
with your horn,
with your howl.

Advent

There's no track as such, but an oak or lime
points a witch's finger or twisted limb
like an old sign, and this flank of river
curves like a road – wet mud metalled by sun –
with the tide at sea, off fishing for crabs.
Night's backcloth pinned to the sky with sharp stars,
all the calendar's windows open wide
and alive with Advent: time now to rise,
to strike out with clenched heart and no map
bar the view from the peak, as the west wind
pummels your face, leads with its granite fists.
Days of rain, rain that permeates the bone,
personal rain persecuting the soul, days
when the promised lake is a dishwater pond
wrung from a grey cloud onto a dead hill.
Drink from your hand through the sieve of your teeth,
eat what the rook or crow leaves on its plate,
bed down where even the fox wouldn't sleep.
Till the way narrows and halts, and you wait
in armour or anorak under the ridge
with a campfire tan and hedgerow hair,
and a god looks down, wordless, stony-faced,
bearded with living moss. This is the place,
the journey over and the story told,
the yarn at the end of its long green thread.

Speak now for all that you're worth, as the blade
swoons in judgement over your pretty head.

Ever Fallen In Love With Someone
(You Shouldn't't've)

To be at the front. To ride that sweetspot
where the crowd lifts like the swell of the sea
under the harbour wall. Just for an hour
to be one ten-thousandth of the whole piece,
lost in the incense and piss, loving the mosh
and the flags and the fists, re-enacting the war.

But the headline band takes to the main stage
and a fever swims in your eight-year-old blood,
so we're acres away, pinned in a tent,
the tent itself all membrane and fine net
taking the drum's pulse, trawling the air
for the twang of the bass and the singer's voice,
and you sleep now in the curtained light,
your face like the face in the back of a spoon,
my lips to yours but for the merest breadth,
mouthing the words, living your every breath.

The Watchman's Speech

When will the Gods release me from the night,
scanning the rim of the earth to the east
looking for fire, tethered here like a dog
on the palace roof for a full year?

I've learned to read the sky's disc as it turns:
which stars are fruitseed, which are seeds of rain,
when they rise and set, what they mean to men.
But the true task is to watch for the torch
that spells the fall of Troy, then wake the Queen
and see the flames reflecting in her eyes,
ignite a fire-storm in the Queen's mind.

This bedroll of mine is sodden with dew,
like a sheet from a sickbed, steeped in sweat;
and Fear, not Sleep, puts its lips to my ear,
so my eyes snap open at every noise,
and should some old song well up in my throat
then I weep for this house, all creaks and groans,
which was once a temple of trust and grace.
You Gods, let the metal shield of the moon
strike the mountain's flint. Send me a sign.

But wait now, look how the horizon burns –
too early for dawn, too near for a star –
a beacon to kickstart this dead city
into a lively dance. I'll rouse the Queen
so she might rise and give thanks. In fact
I'll do a little old victory jig myself
now the snake eyes of the dice lie face down.

And I'll make the King's good fortune my own,
grasp in my hands the bronze hilt of his arm
when the King comes striding out of the glow.

The walls of this palace, if they could talk,
could tell a tale or two. For my own part,
I wink and whisper with those in the know,
but to those who know nothing I'm blank and dumb,
just a watchman, and a great ox squats on my tongue.

Diana and Actaeon

The whole hillside being smeared and daubed
with the blood of the hunt, I dropped down
to a stream whose water ran clear and cool,
and followed its thread through a wooded fold,
among branches dressed with pelts and skulls.
Then stumbled headlong into that sacred grove.

That's when the universe pitched and groaned,
and I shrank from cloud-coloured flesh,
from calf and hip, curve and cleft,
from a writhing feast of fruit and meat:
salmon, silverside, redcurrant, peach;
from fingers worming for gowns and robes,
from eel and oyster, ankle and lip,
from bulb, bud, honeycomb, nest . . . And flinched

from Diana's arm bent back like a bow,
and flinched from Diana's naked glare –
a death-stare arrowed from eye to eye.
All seen in a blink but burnt on the mind.

Drawn back, the pink-red curtain of noon
unleashes the white wolves of the moon.

Getting lost in the Cheviots in the drizzle and fog, on only the second day, was a miserable, unsettling experience and a taste of things to come. The poem bubbled up out of a sense of relief, having finally stumbled across a wooden post with the Pennine Way icon carved into it. Hare's-tail cottongrass is especially emblematic of northern moorland, but oddly incongruous as well, the woolly tufts flaring brilliantly white and delicate against the imposing, sombre landscape and (on that day) the sullen weather. Like tea-lights at the side of the path, and eventually like a forgotten or archaic population, they were my only company for several hours.

Cottongrass

Hand-maidens, humble courtiers,
yes-men in silver wigs,
you stoop low at the path's edge, bow
to the military parade
of boot and stick.

Then it's back to the work,
to the acid acres.
To wade barefoot through waterlogged peat,

trawling the breeze, carding the air
for threads of sheep-wool snagged on the breeze.

Letting time blaze through your ageless hair
like the wind.

*

High Cup Gill is sometimes described as 'the English Grand Canyon', but I only caught glimpses of its long, steep-sided abyss during momentary breaches in the low cloud. On the plateau beyond, close to an out-of-bounds area of M.O.D. land and before the bridge over Maize Beck, a dark and sodden horse or 'fell pony' suddenly appeared out of the mist, followed by several more, dragging all their history and folklore with them. They live wild on the hills, in all weather, and struck me as unreal, mythical creatures, especially in the way they emerged then melted away, and did so entirely noiselessly.

Fell Ponies

They have got up
out of the dirt, the first
hauling the buried boat or ramshackle cart
of its own self

from a ditch.
Then four more follow,
the props of their legs
fossilized limbs of oak,

because there were forests here once.
Not ponies as we know them
but big-engined,
an early design,

leather straps and hardwood cogs
at work when they move,
boulders for ballast
swinging in rope sacks

strung from a crude frame,
the flesh
an all-over daub
of soil and mulch that won't set.

But a lean burn all the same –
just enough breath
on the oil
to keep the lamp in flame . . .

All this gone wild,
Ashington escapees grown moody and mean
on aloneness and sleet.
They trundle forward

into some old war, then forget,
or blink awake from a dream
of pack road or pit,
of ploughs or sleds

at their heels,
then lower their heads

to browse on root and weed.
Wherever they halt

is the world's edge,
or they wait
just an inch from the future's wall of glass,
seeing nothing,

taking it all in, at any moment
to turn into mist, or re-emerge,
come lumbering
out of the flooded mine,

now cut-outs up on the ridge,
now barring the path to the bridge,
seaweed fringes and axe-head stares,
their hides

knotted rugs of rags
slung over the beam of the spine,
all smoke and steam,
ignited by lightning strike in the first storm,

put out by rain.

*

On some of the lower-lying arable land in the North
Pennines, owners are being encouraged and subsidised
to sow hay meadows in place of the more usual winter-
fodder crops. The different varieties of wild flowers result
in further biodiversity among birds, insects and other

wildlife, and are also prettier on the eye. One species making a comeback under this policy is yellow rattle, or 'poverty', traditionally thought of as a pest by farmers. The poem begins as a kind of field-note then riffs on a list of the flower's common names, many of which 'spoke to me' as an itinerant poet singing for his supper.

Yellow Rattle (Poverty)

Hairless, leaves unstalked, toothed.
Two-lipped, lower lip decurved.
Calyx distended in fruit. Semi-parasite,

throws itself on the parish,
gets its hooks into good roots.
A beggar to shift

once it gains a toe-hold.
Bad-mouthed by farm-folk.
Goes among meadows, grassy places.

Hard times, one by the verge,
hunched, cap in hand,
shaking the poor-box, the husk

of its see-through purse
in its see-through fingers,
dry-voiced, whispering

spare any change, sir,
a penny for Fiddlecase,
a penny for Shacklebasket,
penny for old Hayshackle, sir,
help poor Pots 'n' Pans,
a penny for Rattle Jack,
spare a few pence for old Pepperbox, sir,
a penny for Cockscomb,
a ha'penny for old Hen Penny, sir,
remember old Shepherd's Coffin,
remember poor Snaffles,
a penny for Poverty, sir, most kindly,

when I brush past,
when I breeze through,
when I swish by.

*

Setting out one morning from Ickornshaw heading towards Top Withens and Brontë country, I passed a series of sinister-looking out-buildings on the first hillside. Some people hiking with me said they were private lodges for the annual grouse shoots, another man said they were vacation 'chalets' used by locals at weekends and during the summer. It seemed improbable that anyone would consider that stretch of bleak and exposed terrain to be a holiday destination worthy of a 'beach hut', even if one part of the moor is named on the map as 'The Sea'. All the huts were locked, with their windows blacked out, and decidedly unwelcoming except to the prying imagination.

Above Ickornshaw, Black Huts

are raised against damp
on footings of red brick,
landlocked chalets lashed to the bedrock

with steel guy-ropes
and telegraph wire,
braced for Atlantic gales.

All plank and slat,
the salvaged timbers
ooze bitumen

out of the grain, a liquorice sweat,
its formaldehyde breath
disinfecting the clough

for a mile downwind.
Seen from distance,
these tarred pavilions or lodges

make camp on the ridge
in silhouette – black, identical sheds
of identical shape,

though up close
no two are alike,
being customised shacks,

a hillbilly hotchpotch
of water-butts, stoops,
a one-man veranda,

a stove-pipe wearing a tin hat.
And all boarded shut,
all housing

a darkroom darkness,
with pin-hole light
falling on nail or hook

or a padlocked box,
coffin-shaped, coiled
in a ship's chain.

Mothballed stations on disused lines
neither mapped nor named.
Birds avoid them –

some say the hatches fly open
and shotguns appear, blazing
at tame grouse,

that inside
they're all whisky and smoke,
all Barbour and big talk,

but others whisper
that locals sit here
in deckchairs, with flasks,

watching the dunes of peat,
binoculars raised,
waiting for downed airmen

or shipwrecked souls
to crawl
from the moor's sea.

WALKING AWAY

At the end of Braunton Burrows – a very disorientating area of sand dunes, scrubby copses, golf fairways and intersecting tracks – the South West Coast Path veers inland towards crossing points on the Taw and Torridge rivers. Appledore, the next seaside destination, looks tantalisingly close on the other side of the estuary. Heading upstream towards Braunton I saw what looked like a black and yellow necklace draped on a flat stone on a low wall in the afternoon sun, before it slithered into the grass. I'd never seen an adder before, and as an agent of temptation it presented itself at exactly the right hour. I wrote the poem that night, in the graveyard-garden of a converted chapel in Swimbridge.

Adder

Harlequin watch-strap, Pringle sock,
selling itself
on Braunton Burrows, where dry land baulks.

Spineless spine, on its shoulderless
shoulders
all of England's slurs and lies.

The channel here runs deep
and fast, but
wing it, it lisps, *just cut across,*

you could easily save yourself
miles of slog.
Between the electrodes of its tongue

a bridgeable gap, and barely a cockstride
shore to shore
from the edge of the world to Appledore.

*

As someone who grew up and continues to live in a part of Britain which is uncompromisingly inland, I'd been determined to write a poem about the sea. I even thought of such a poem as an inevitability, considering how the sea would be my constant travelling companion for days on end, always there at my right hand side. But I couldn't find the right vocabulary or any point of entry into the poem. Eventually I went back to basics in the form of Ted Hughes's *Poetry in the Making*. In the chapter 'Writing About Landscape' he advises against literal observation in favour of sensual responses: what a thing *feels* like, or what it would feel like to *be* that thing. My own tiredness undoubtedly had a bearing on the outcome.

From Where I Stand

What is the sea?
    The sea is sleep.
Dog-headed fish and transparent
salt-blooded creatures loll and glide

in its depths. Boneless life-forms
turn inside-out in its dreams but it sleeps.

Who is the sea?
      A sleeper, asleep.
Hurricanes rake at its back, the full moon
drags it along by its hair, forked lightning
prongs at its flesh and it won't wake.
Not dead, then, not yet, but asleep.

When is the sea?
      Whenever we sleep.
In the morning look back from the shore
at its sheets, wet with the piss and sweat
of the night, the tide at work laundering
sleep from its sleep with its sleep.

Where is the sea?
      Wherever you sleep.
Walk to the edge where tired waves
snore on the shingle beach, leave
your wallet and phone on a rock, wade
up to your neck. Go under. Be sleep.

Why is the sea?
      Because it sleeps.
Sleeps like a drunk, its feet on the pillow
of reefs and shallows, its head where light
never breaks, face down in the sand.
I know this. I know this, I am the land.

*

I've written dozens of poems about crossing or trying to cross or failing to cross bodies of water, and there's probably a very persuasive Freudian explanation for this. I'd been advised not to attempt to cross the Hayle Estuary, where the current is strong and the water deep and cold, even though the alternative is to walk an extra three miles, some of it on a busy trunk road and through a small industrial estate. In fact the cousins who gave me the advice also offered to canoe me across the mouth, but never turned up on the day. The poem is an acknowledgement of one man's failure of nerve and imagination compared with the bravery and ingenuity of more adventurous travellers, and was partly composed while reluctantly tramping the additional distance.

Legends of the Crossings

One man conquered the estuary's swell
in a scallop shell
that had served as an ash tray,
another canoed on a fallen ash tree.
One woman crossed in the dimpled sloop
of an ice-cream scoop,
or was it a soup ladle
with butter-knife rudder and teaspoon paddle?
Two surfer dudes rolled in from abroad
surfing ironing boards.
Fused at the hip, conjoined twins
rode shotgun on the pectoral fins
of a freshwater porpoise;

a willing Galapagos tortoise
ferried their oversize luggage bank to bank.
A cockler sank
then rose then sank then rose and rose
on the whiskery tip of a grey seal's nose.
Some Michael rowed
his boat ashore, some Jesus strode
the unwalkable ford, a widow scattered
her husband's ashes
into the raging burn
then wobbled home in the empty urn,
and a jilted bride
forged a perfectly good flotation device
from her ex-fiancé's everyday lies,
which were watertight.
A church cross, hewn from a single dogwood trunk
was raft enough for a bearded monk:
a marooned shipmate simply waited
for winter, then simply skated.
Fleeing dune to dune,
a refugee played a comical tune
on the xylophonic stepping stones
of a dead whale's bones,
and a saintly young thing voyaged land to land –
get this – in her own cupped hand
and didn't sink.
But look, our pedestrian stalls at the salty brink
with his waterproof hat and holly stick
and chickens out. He bottles it.

*

Rather than rounding the point after reaching Land's End, I got on a ferry. I'd identified the Isles of Scilly as the last viable place to give a poetry reading on that particular compass bearing, and also hoped to walk between three of the islands at low tide, aiming to finish the journey on unpopulated Samson. To outsiders the Scillies are other-worldly: slow-paced and quaint by some measures, innocent perhaps and idyllic in places, but also elemental, spiritual, disorientating and mysterious. I felt both free and confined on the islands, both hidden and conspicuous, a state of uncertainty heightened by the combination of elation and exhaustion I experienced at nearing the finishing line and looking beyond.

Scillonia

The locals move the hills around at night.
A stone armada moors in the harbour at low tide.
Sleep with an open hand and a dunnock
nests in the palm, raises its young.
Lord Harold lounges in his beachside grave,
eye sockets full of the west, pink sea thrift
crowning his skull, an acetylene wand
of purple agapanthus in his fossil fist.
This crossroads shrine is in fact a shop:
a bowl of eggs, six carrots, an honesty box.
Looking down, the stars see constellations
in the firmament of lights and buoys.
Samson's castaway snuffs out his hurricane lamp
then slides in his tomb. Along the verge,
a dozen blonde narcissi are walking to school.

The Lives of the Poets

They rise early, just after lunchtime.
Their breath on the mirror confirms their existence.
They should rest a while, but today is crunch time

for a rhyme that stands between now and forever,
time to knuckle down to some monkey business.
They sharpen a quill and pause for a breather.

How they hero worship those quarantined villagers
who nursed the plague and paid for provisions
with small coins purged in saucers of vinegar.

Because suffering helps; if things get too cosy a
sugary residue coats the tongue,
hence the grinding of peppercorns into Ambrosia.

Late afternoon, and for meaning or moral
they stand at the window and gaze towards yonder,
at the forked oak or a bird in the laurel,

but their compound vision plays tricks by the hundred:
in the clenched fist they notice the rosebud,
in the pretty rose they see Joe Bugner.

They have pinned their hopes on the incidental:
the sky might be falling, but look at these plums
or this red wheelbarrow. They offer so little,

expect even less, and a plaque on their houses
is ample reward for the faffing and fiddling,
for the inky stains on their big girls' blouses,

for the shuffling and scratching, for occasionally traipsing
up to the post box or lagging behind us
and pulling faces. Mimicking. Aping.

IN MEMORY OF WATER

THE SNOW STONE

Pule Hill stoops over the village of Marsden where I was born and brought up. Its rounded, bald head sits in a landscape of smoother, more expansive moorland and elevated reservoirs; it serves as a kind of homecoming beacon after trips away and signals the beginning or the end of Yorkshire across that particular Pennine crossing, depending on the direction of travel. Away from the summit, about halfway along a west-facing ridge, there's a disused quarry, which felt very primitive and pagan when I first walked into it as a child, and still has a peculiar, melancholy atmosphere. I once found snow in the quarry at Easter time, a deep drift that the sun hadn't managed to shift, and the poem tries to capture and celebrate the transformative power of snow and its cleansing effect on the senses. In such weather, Close Moss on the other side of the A62 becomes a blank page, and there's now a 'poetry seat' near the carved poem inviting visitors to sit, think, compose. The snow poem is written laterally at about eye-level across two slabs that formed part of a crude roofless building or shelter in the quarrying era.

Snow

The sky has delivered
its blank missive.
The moor in coma.
Snow, like water asleep,
a coded muteness
to baffle all noise,
to stall movement,
still time.
What can it mean
that colourless water
can dream
such depth of white?
We should make the most
of the light.

Stars snag
on its crystal points.
The odd, unnatural pheasant
struts and slides.
Snow, snow, snow
is how the snow speaks,
is how its clean page reads.
Then it wakes, and thaws,
and weeps.

*

After walking the Pennine Way in 2010, one of my abiding memories concerns the sudden appearance of Greater Manchester, which came steaming into view as I headed south along the service track from Stoodley Pike monument towards Blackstone Edge Reservoir. The view then extends beyond the sprawling conurbation of east Lancashire to include the Welsh mountains, the disc of Jodrell Bank radio telescope and Winter Hill mast above Bolton. Cow's Mouth Quarry seems to stand with its jaws open, agog at those prevailing weather systems which come barrelling across the Atlantic then unload against the first hills that stand in their way. I first visited the carved poem in a downpour, when the letters appeared to be weeping flames, water pouring from the raw letters which were golden in colour, or the colour of honeycomb toffee. The rain stone is part of a natural outcrop on the far side of a drainage ditch, and can be see from the platform of the path for those who keep walking, or used a backrest for those who prefer to stop and gaze toward the Americas.

Rain

Be glad
of these freshwater tears,
each pearled droplet
some salty old sea-bullet
air-lifted out of the waves,
then laundered and sieved,

recast as a soft bead
and returned.

And no matter how much
it strafes or sheets,
it is no mean feat
to catch one raindrop
clean in the mouth,
to take one drop
on the tongue, tasting
cloud-pollen,
grain of the heavens,
raw sky.

Let it teem, up here
where the front of the mind
distils
the brunt of the world.

*

THE MIST STONE

The land below Nab Hill falls away steeply toward the
village of Oxenhope, toward Brontë Country and ultimately
toward North Yorkshire. A shallow reservoir shivers to the
west, and behind it stand several wind turbines, sometimes
static and unnerving but more often cart-wheeling manically
in the streaming air. So the immediate environment speaks
of human intervention, and that theme continues with the
quarry workings or 'delphs' either side of the east-running
path, through the tyre-tread of trail bikes in the peat and

mud, and through the presence of several Goldsworthy-style cairns or installations assembled by anonymous land-artists and standing tall and mysterious along the escarpment. I didn't want the mist stone to compete or interfere with those furtively constructed forms, so the poem is carved into a flat-lying slab that actually broke in half while being manoeuvred into position, giving the piece the feel of two facing pages within a book or codex. The poem describes the kind of ecstatic fear that comes from being entirely enveloped by mist. The last phrase, 'you are here' seeks to mimic the language of the town map and reinforce the miracle of existence in the same breath.

Mist

Who does it mourn?
What does it mean,
such nearness,
gathering here
on high ground
while your back was turned,
drawing its net curtains around?
Featureless silver screen, mist
is water
in its ghost state,
all inwardness,
holding its milky breath,
veiling the pulsing machines
of great cities
under your feet,

walling you
into these moments,
into this anti-garden
of gritstone and peat.

Given time
the edge of your being
will seep
into its fibreless fur;
you are lost, adrift
in hung water and blurred air,
but you are here.

*

THE DEW STONES

The two dew stones stand upright in an old gate-hole in a
dry-stone wall, and the narrow serrated gap between them
encourages the prying eye, like peering through a curtain
or partially opened door. Beyond is a view of fields and
farms that rises to the far horizon, a worked landscape
quite different from the moorland locations which host
the sister stones. The pine forest before the poem is an
artificial creation and at some stage in the future will be
felled for timber, but for now it offers a dark and silent
approach under an interlocking green canopy and along
paths muffled and carpeted by fallen needles. I wanted to
evoke the still and jewelled dawn, when the battles of the
previous day and the terrors of night have been soothed or
eased by morning dew. Dew as a peacemaker or emollient,
especially at the end of those old-fashioned summers when
the moors seemed ready to erupt into fire at the slightest

spark or wrong word. Precipitation in its gentlest, subtlest
form, but with each droplet like a three hundred and sixty
degree microscope or a tiny liquid world.

Dew

The tense stand-off
of summer's end,
the touchy fuse-wire
of parched grass,
tapers of bulrush and reed,
any tree
a primed mortar
of tinder, one spark
enough to trigger
a march on the moor
by ranks of flame.

Dew enters the field
under cover of night,
tending the weary and sapped,
lifting its thimble of drink
to the lips of a leaf,
to the stoat's tongue,
trimming a length of barbed-wire fence
with liquid gems, here
where bog-cotton
flags its surrender
or carries its torch
for the rain.

Then dawn, when sunrise
plants its fire-star
in each drop, ignites
each trembling eye.

*

THE PUDDLE STONE

The humble puddle might be thought of as the runt of the
rain family but I wanted to attribute a greater significance
to it. The poem is carved in two stanzas divided between
a pair of horizontally bedded flagstones or 'causey paving'
which form part of a path between the Thimble Stones and
the trig point which leads towards the swollen summit of
Ilkley Moor. That moor, and the encompassing Rombalds
Moor, provided both inspiration and justification for the
whole Stanza Stones project, being home to an uncountable
number of standing stones, carved stones and other pre-
historic markings that testify to humanity's desire to make
communicative gestures in wild and remote places. In the
puddle poem, sunlight or global warming becomes a kind
of narcissism, and an environmental theme suggests itself
more boldly here than elsewhere, the cautionary tone of
the piece referring back to the overall title for this suite of
poems, *In Memory of Water*. Unlike the other five Stanza
Stones, these two look to me like graves.

Puddle

Rain-junk.
Sky-litter.
Some May mornings
Atlantic storm-horses
clatter this way,
shedding their iron shoes
in potholes and ruts,
shoes that melt
into steel-grey puddles
then settle and set
into cloudless mirrors
by noon.

The shy deer
of the daytime moon
comes to sip from the rim.
But the sun
likes the look of itself,
stares all afternoon,
its hard eye
lifting the sheen
from the glass,
turning the glaze
to rust.
Then we don't see things
for dust.

*

The stone is a squat, Buddha-like boulder in Backstone Beck, the narrow creek running from the lipped plateau of Ilkley Moor towards Cowpasture Road and the town of Ilkley itself. Despite being only twenty yards or so from a well-used footpath and not far from the tourist trap of the Cow and Calf rocks the poem isn't easy to locate, tucked away in a dog-leg in the stream, hidden behind a patch of brambles on one side and a bank of exposed shale on the other, the valley becoming a steep ravine towards its upper reaches. But once found there's a grassy promontory that serves as a viewing point, and to stand and read the poem can be a dizzying experience, the curved surface of the stone making the lines flex and swirl, the fast-running waters of the beck pouring and eddying to each side of the text. Occasionally the volume of water means that the lower edges of the poem are almost unreadable, and given the volatility of current weather conditions it's possible that at some point the boulder itself will be rolled or flushed away. But that's true of all the poems; they may be written in stone but the element they describe will eventually render them mute.

Beck

It is all one chase.
Trace it back: the source
might be nothing more
than a teardrop
squeezed from a curlew's eye,

then follow it down
to the full-throated roar
at its mouth:
a dipper
strolls the river
dressed for dinner
in a white bib.

The unbroken thread
of the beck
with its nose for the sea,
all flux and flex,
soft-soaping a pebble
for over a thousand years,
or here
after hard rain
sawing the hillside in half
with its chain.
Or here,
where water unbinds
and hangs
over the waterfall's face,
and just for that one
stretched white moment
becomes lace.

Zodiac T-Shirt

The avenues marching
with combat shorts,
the pavements strutting
with micro-skirts.

No rest from the sun,
a smothering heat
like a mother beast
asleep on its young.

> *Zodiac T-shirt,*
> *paper-clip bracelet,*
> *mercury rising,*
> *call in the crash-team.*

Knock for knock
and tit for tat,
your bike got nicked
so you nicked one back.

We pull up a tree
and plant a rose,
where a cigarette dies,
another one grows.

> *Zodiac T-shirt,*
> *paper-clip bracelet,*
> *mercury rising,*
> *call in the crash-team.*

Hand in hand
when the bendi-bus stopped,
a couple got on,
a couple got off,

and an ice-cream wept
on the steps of the church
and the crusted-up reservoir
died of thirst.

>   *Zodiac T-shirt,*
>   *paper-clip bracelet,*
>   *mercury rising,*
>   *call in the crash-team.*

Drink for drink
in the park that night,
me scratching yours,
you scratching mine,

till the words came thumping
hand over fist,
and the sky blew a fuse
and it started to piss

>   *on your Zodiac T-shirt,*
>   *paper-clip bracelet,*
>   *crucifix pendant,*
>   *cinnamon toothpaste,*
>   *chewing-gum pavement,*
>   *liquorice protest,*
>   *dragonfly heartbeat,*
>   *daisy-chain necklace,*

candy-stripe shoelace,
fingerbob Jesus,
pregnancy dipstick,
all back to your place,
body-bag suitcase,
mercury rising,
cardiac jump-leads,
call in the crash-team, call in the crash-team,
call in the crash-team, call in the crash-team.

THE GREAT WAR — AN ELEGY

Sea Sketch

Dear Mother, I have come to the sea
    to wash my eyes
in its purples, blues, indigos, greens,

to enter its world and emerge cleansed,
    to break the surface
then watch the surface heal and mend.

Behind me the land lies mauled and wrenched,
    but I have not flinched
from uncommon holes in the flesh of men

or heads oozing with shattered minds,
    and have not shied
from livers and lungs exposed to the light,

and have balanced and carried faltering hearts
    in my cupped hands
through the egg and spoon race of death and life.

Some men I kissed: boy soldiers
    raving and blind,
begging for love from a mother's lips,

and when death stands with its black shawl
    at the foot of the bed
a white cotton handkerchief eases the soul . . .

So allow me the beach, the sea,
    its handwritten waves,
the act of making a simple sketch

of a simple ketch, or stick figures plunging
    into the depths,
or a cormorant baring its breast to the sun,

or at dusk, Venus robed in her wedding dress,
    her silver train
like a path on the water heading west.

Remains

The faint of heart
won't want to trawl
through a mud-bath strewn
with body-parts:
an architect's hand,
a surgeon's rib,
an explorer's foot
still laced in its boot,
the flaxen shock
of an actor's hair,
an artist's eye,
a composer's ear,
a philosopher's skull,
a glass-blower's lungs ,
an inventor's spine,
a poet's tongue.

A century on
that soil still bleeds
and earth yields up
unholy growths
of fingernails
and lower jaws
and wisdom teeth
and funny bones,
and Tommy still roams
the fields and lanes

all leaden-limbed,

all hollow-voiced,

all vacant-looking,

all bullet-brained,

all never-was,

all might-have-been.

Considering the Poppy

Consider the poppy.
Think it a life,
the plasma and milk
of its petals and stalk.

Or think it a face,
the agonised blush,
blood vessels flushed
with revulsion, pain.

Think it an eye:
the bloodshot iris
and ink-black pit
staring blank and blind,

or think it a mouth,
muted, stunned,
or think it a flag,
planted there

flying nobody's colours
in no-man's land.
Or think it a soul,
the fallen, lost,

or think it a hole,
the gaping nought
of an entry wound
or exit wound.

Or think it a ghost,
or think it a heart.
But above all
think it a thought:

a seed of thought
that might sleep in the mind

for a hundred years
then sprout and bud

and blossom and fruit,
a memory bubble
that blooms in the brain,
a Rorschach smudge

or crimson stain
that reminds and reminds
when it flares and flames.
So consider the poppy,

pinned on a blouse
or pinned on a coat,
or growing wild
among corn and kale,

and recall and recall.

Lazarus

Only the dead inhabit the dust and roots.
And that concrete step bearing down on the soil
was a tombstone under a sentry's boots.
Yet here is a miracle, here is a soul
with a chisel and breadknife, worming his way
through acres of underworld, breaking the earth
one moonless night to emerge *like the risen* . . .
. . . then vanish completely into a field of rye.

Then emerge once more, this time a vision
with dirt in his fingernails, mud in his hair,
breathing England's air to the depths of his lungs,
tasting English words on the tip of his tongue,
and that glinting, flickering point of light
at the tunnel's end still alive in his eyes.

In Avondale

That isn't the way the coalman knocks
– dark earth and blackened hands –
who rattles the letterbox?

That isn't the way the milkman knocks
– white flesh strewn in foreign lands –
who rattles the letterbox?

That isn't the way the fish-seller knocks
– open mouthed, staring eyes –
who rattles the letter box?

That isn't the way the egg-man knocks
– cracked shells and broken lives –
who rattles the letterbox?

So a mother buttons her first son's coat
in Avondale, in Avondale,
and his name comes home in an envelope.

And a mother buttons her second son's coat
and wraps a muffler around his throat
in Avondale, in Avondale,
and his name comes home in an envelope.

And runs a comb through her third son's fringe
and wipes a crumb from her fourth son's lips
and presses a note in her fifth son's fist
in Avondale, in Avondale,
and buttons their coats
and their names come home in envelopes.

Some days
the wind troubles the hinges and locks
and the sunflower sways and the tree-house rocks
but it's deadly quiet in Avondale when somebody knocks.
Who rattles, who rattles the letterbox?

The Thankful

So farmhands trundle their carts and horses
past barley fields and oak-wood copses,

among them, wagoner Arthur Brown,
driving his team

in a simple world
of rolling hills and folded wolds,

through an open gate at the edge of the heath
into hell on earth.

What country is this, where lanes and furrows
are trenches, lines and running sewers,

where a blackthorn hedge
is barbed wire flowered with hair and flesh,

where ripening wheat and wind-ruffled grass
are the bloom and sway of poison gas,

that mustardy mist
through which

farmhands trundle their wagons and horses . . .
. . . ghostly hearses.

But they counted them out then counted them home,
every one, and there among them Arthur Brown,

pipe smoke drifting into the clouds,
reins in his hands,

steering his team
up the long and narrow tree-lined lane

from war and battle
into corn and cattle.

Memorial

I wage no war,
carry no fight. I have
no bone to pick
or axe to grind.

I've never been
the battle type,
though army medals
hang like moons

or chocolate sovereigns
from a cousin's breast,
and uncles
on my father's side

drove mules and donkeys
up the line
and tasted gas
and slept in mud.

No child of mine
will deal in blood
or play with guns.
I have no sons.

But of those legions
called to die,
build them a cenotaph
that chimes:

as long as there's
a willing hand
to point the walls
and fettle moss

from chiselled names,
as long as there's
a living soul
to wind the coils

and oil the cogs
and grease the rods,
and passers by
to count the strike

of bronze on bronze,
what better way
to monumentalise
the dead and lost

within the clockwork
of the mind
than honour them
with stone and time.

In Praise of Air

I write in praise of air. I was six or five
when a conjurer opened my knotted fist
and I held in my palm the whole of the sky.
I've carried it with me ever since.

Let air be a major god, its being
and touch, its breast-milk always tilted
to the lips. Both dragonfly and Boeing
dangle in its see-through nothingness . . .

Among the jumbled bric-a-brac I keep
a padlocked treasure-chest of empty space,
and on days when thoughts are fuddled with smog
or civilization crosses the street

with a white handkerchief over its mouth
and cars blow kisses to our lips from theirs
I turn the key, throw back the lid, breathe deep.
My first word, everyone's first word, was air.

Medical Examiner's Office/Three Room Dwelling

An office block
on a downtown street:
to the outside eye
just several storeys

of swivel chairs and computer screens.
And a key. A regular key
for a standard lock.
When opened, the door

doesn't gasp or swoon.
This isn't a mausoleum or tomb.
The visitor here
won't faint or puke.

Yet all that unfolds
in this windowless space
is horribly odd, beautifully chilling,
disturbingly cute,

like a reptile house
of small glass tanks
set into the walls, or Perspex cabinets
standing on plinths,

miniature worlds,
each diorama a micro drama
but stalled in time, each frozen scene
an incubation of proofs and facts.

Take exhibit A:
a three room dwelling
housed in a case. Inside
Kate Judson sleeps

in her six inch bed
on a pillow of blood.
Robert Judson sprawls
face down in the sheets,

the pale blue lines
of his pinstripe pyjamas
blotched with red,
then walk your eyes

from room to room,
past the table set for a family meal,
the tins on the shelves,
the folded tea-towel

hung on the sink,
past the phone on the hook,
the copper kettle asleep on the stove,
the knitted teddy bear

cast aside, past the rifle lying
at five to five on the kitchen floor,

and the small gold husk
of a bullet shell,

and the turned over chair,
to the spattermarks crowning
the nursery wall above the crib,
over Linda Mae's head.

Outside on the porch,
three bottles of milk –
one pint, one pint,
one half a pint – unspilt.

Barn

Whether theatre sets
or murder scenes, whether
science or art,
each piece is the work

of a nerveless calm,
an architect's eye,
an artist's hand,
a singular mind.

Poke a flashlight beam
through the open doors
of this model barn.
Framed by timbers

of seasoned wood
from an actual farm,
poor Eben Wallace
hangs by his neck,

the coarse rope hitched
from a hook on the door jamb,
bottom left,
then over the hay-hoist

and in through the hatch.
The thin wooden crate
couldn't bear his weight,
so he swings

just inches at most
above the floor.
Straw everywhere,
everywhere straw.

Mrs Wallace suggests
he'd made threats before,
but this time has Eben
gone too far?

Those tread marks
made by a tractor tyre –
are they fresh?
An ox yoke leans

against the wall,
a good luck horseshoe
rests on a nail,
sunlight breaks in

through the planks and slats.
Would Eben really
have topped himself?
Hay everywhere, everywhere hay

and somewhere among it
the needle of truth, beneath
that weathervane, or is it
a cross on the roof?

Dark Bathroom

Here's a shabby scene,
a pitiful sight,
a dingy bathroom
half-panelled with wood,

toilet paper in single sheets
on a metal hook
at the side of the loo,
hand-washed underwear strung on a line

from door frame to beam –
you can almost
smell the loneliness,
taste the damp.

Above the tub
the leaded window
and stained glass speak
of faded glory, a past carved up

into bedsits and flats.
What else: naked pipework
runs in and out,
the rain-coloured flannel

behind the tap
is little more than a threadbare rag,
the soap dish offers
a brick of soap.

Something's not right,
the mirror on the wall
isn't hanging straight,
an empty bottle lies skittled and supped

on the tatty rug,
you can almost hear
the voices of men – two men
who came and laughed

and whispered and left,
leaving Maggie Wilson fully dressed
in her knitted slippers, pretty cardi
and lacy skirts

stone cold on her back
in the galvanized bath,
her black-stockinged legs
poking weird and stiffly

over the side, the tap left on,
the water – almost a solid stream – pouring
onto her mouth,
her two blue eyes

looking blank, looking north.
So, what means what?
Can we hazard a guess?
Take a shot in the dark?

The plug's not in, but hangs
like a pocket watch
on a length of chain.
I'd say it was evening time.

Mother and Child

As if from the deep well of myself
I'd hauled him out, little albino cub
with his blank thumb of a face,
as nude as the moon.

My infant yeti, alien pup;
with his paws at my neck
his plump marzipan arms
made a watertight bowl at my breast

where he could wash,
where he could lap at the sea-water I'd wept.
O he was mine alright, pillow-case smooth
but marsupial, strange, papoosed

in otherness, his cheeks
not yet pummelled by lies,
his lips not yet peeled by lies,
his tongue still unborn.

My locked hands made a sling, cupping
his boneless weight,
and I knew without looking
that shadows moved like fish

under his mottled skin,
that his cute birthmarks were my stains.
Soft thoughts idled and nudged
in the globe of his head.

I turned to one side, saying
look at us, joined in the flesh,
formed of a single piece.
Carve us like this.

Odysseus in the Naiads' Cave

So why would a man crash out on a stony floor
after two decades away and now just a stroll
from his wife and home? The long sea-cave disappears
into itself like an ear that listens for war:
the strike of spearhead on shield, blade against bone,
weeks of mundane silence between savage attacks.
Or the cave is a shell full of the ocean's screams,
wind nagging the torn sails and frayed ropes, the din
of hearing himself drown, only to rise again.
His young hound will be grey at the muzzle these days.
His son was one – he'll be tall and bearded by now.
But dressed in a hospital gown, his mind swimming
with blood and brine, he'll bed down on that stony floor
until the eyebright opens and the whitethroat sings.

Women Winding Wool

It's always Sunday in their world,
mid-morning, the breakfast things tidied away,
the lid back on the butter dish,
tea leaves cast on the earth.
There's a fair in town and they'd like to go,
let candyfloss fritter and fry
on their tongues, link arms and skip
through the beery jokes of furnace-faced men,
win a fish in a bowl.
But there's wool to be wound:
one of them widens her arms
to the length of a carp – the one that got away –
the other tugs at the line,
trawling for lugs and knots.
A real fire glazes the walls to a brick-dust red.
A clock tut-tuts on the mantelpiece.

With their swimmers' shoulders and strong backs
they're no shirkers, these two,
but the world perishes, wanes. Their porcelain faces
pale and craze. Decades ago those housecoats
were ball gowns; look at them now,
faded to pleats, seams, tacking stitch, tailor's chalk,
a few gold threads. Fabric sheers to nothingness
over the bald hills of their knees.

A gentleman caller came once,
his heart in his mouth, his mother's engagement ring
burning a hole in his fist . . .
But there's wool to be wound,

wood and brass to be polished,
life to be kept taut on its long chain.
Later, they might open a small tin of salmon for tea.

Large Reclining Figure

'Large' I'll accept but 'reclining' my shiny white arse
I'm like crouched I'm like ready to pounce I'm like
c'mon LET'S GO ask anyone who's got up close and personal
who's eyeballed the cats' ears of my breasts
the shoulder pads (kind of) of my breasts
who's seen the antennae ready and up!
Check out the bling, pearlescent raindrops like . . . raindrops
on a new car, and me the colour
of v. expensive anti-wrinkle cream slash face pack
made of minerals dredged from deep earth, because sometimes
you've got to squeeze geology for all it's worth, right?
Today, let's call it a Wednesday, I'm channelling
Apple Mac hardware meets skin-tight lycra meets Sinclair C5
meets the King's Road circa blah blah blah,
oh and I'm casually throwing a pashmina of sunlight
over my arched back with woodland appliqué
by way of reflections and formal garden detail ie
manicured yew hedge and espaliered apple tree as seen
through my HOLES. Truly, girls, which of yous
wouldn't kill for calves like mine or
an ankle like this even if I do sorta tail off
into anchor or big tooth
even if my southern end goes a bit mermaid on me
like sperm in champagne, so what? Pelvic,

I've heard people say. My reply: don't stand by the door
like I'm some starched old duchess draped on a chaise longue,
get up here, mister, and take a whiff I smell of nothing
it's the new black, and while you're round there
what's that submarine hatch porthole letterbox thing
in my hind-part – go figure – there's God knows what in there
could be my secret Tipp-Ex stash could be
a foxhole I don't have eyes in the back of my *ahem* 'head'
but quit knocking on the paintwork, kid, I don't like
the hollow I am. The void.
Hey, flies daren't even land they're these
itty bitty spacecraft buzzin' round the mother-of-all
mother-ships in some eighties sci-fi flick.
Never seen a <u>me</u> before? You should
get outside more throw back the flaps
of the oxygen tent put the iron lung in the wardrobe
taste the prevailing winds that whistle through my cavities.
Or call me, yeah? Call me. You'll be like
darling you were marvellous
the camera loves you kiss kiss kiss and I'll be like
give me my own @ my own # my own show for chrissake
just give me my own channel I'm not
getting out of bed for anything less.

The Underground

In Book XI of Homer's *Odyssey*, the battle-weary
and storm-smashed Ulysses visits the Land of the Dead,
sails where black poplars loom like charred masts,

sails on through the trailing creepers of lachrymose willows
whose fruits never ripen but die young on the branch,

then beaches his sea-worn boat on a gravel shore
where a river of fire and a river of tears curdle and twist.
On a spit of land he pours honey, milk and wine into a pit,
mixes in water and grain, and bleeds and burns a black ewe
and a black ram, as instructed, then waits for ghosts.

And there we find him in his matinee idol suit,
in the film noir of wartime London, sketchbook in hand.
The living are shrouded in bedspreads, curtains or long coats.
Some line the platform, as if laid out, others are camped
on the hard stone steps, stage right, under a sword of light.

In the dark tunnel, stage left, the dead are rousing themselves.
And not just the old: young brides with their wedding posies
clamped in their fists, unmarried men, nameless infants,
great battalions of bloodied soldiers in military dress
still with their spears raised or bayonets fixed.

Friends, loved ones, world leaders and guttersnipes,
all stirring now from as far as Acton Town or Baron's Court,
drawn by the whisper of charcoal on paper, the scratch
of pencil on page, so many restless, see-through souls
lured to the cave's mouth, brought to the brink

by Ulysses in his ironed white shirt, smart shoes, knotted tie,
his fingers cupping a few candelas, a few lumens of light.
Over his shoulder his shadow looks on, admiring
the shading and draughtsmanship, the two of them leaning
against a wall that stands between that world and this.

Woman

My mother was copper,
her mother
was copper as well. We go

far back,
sieved from rivers
or ground from earth.

Pure redheads by birth
they dull our blood
with cartwheels, cannonballs,

any old iron;
the green comes later
like a hard moss.

Cast and recast
I inhabited
coins, fuse wire,

Mycenae spearheads,
beakers and pots,
but was mesmerised

to catch a glimpse
of my latest form
in the polished glaze

of a gallery door,
all torso and neck
with a swollen heart

under my left breast,
the eyes of my nipples
staring back, transfixed

by hollows and curves,
by these tribal scars
and amputee knees,

by the swept hair
exposing
a wounded skull.

Then blushed at the thought
of his bare hands
on my raw cheeks

and between my legs
as he moulded
and shaped. I ask this:

if he touched his lips
against mine
then closed my mouth

with a smear of his thumb,
did that
count as love?

On the Existing State of Things

from Virgil, The Aeneid, Book VI

> Then to those shores
that Charon patrols, stalking the quayside,
haunting beach and bay, harbourmaster and ferryman.
With a straggly grey beard under his bloodshot eyes
and a money bag slung from his bony shoulder
he tacks and jibes, tunes the outboard motor,
herding his cargo into a rusty hull,
old in years but a tireless God of the grave.

Here a pitiful mob crowded the strand:
husbands and wives, the drained dishevelled forms
of the once-proud, bewildered children,
pale daughters and sons pulled from rubble and ash,
men and women holed by sniper rounds.

So many souls, countless as dry leaves
loosened by frost, spinning through autumn woods,
or like flocking birds that darken a clear sky,
migrating seaward looking for greener worlds.
They lined the banks begging to be next to cross,
arms stretched towards a distant coast.
But Charon trafficked as he pleased, first these, then those,
ordering others to stand back from the boat.

. . .

And there among them the ghost of Palinurus.
Sailing at night from Libya, piloting north,
transfixed by tail lights bound for Munich and Heathrow

he'd slipped from the stern and gone down in the wake.
Seeing his mournful shape among those shades
Aeneas called out, 'Palinurus, answer me;
which God tipped the Mediterranean into your lungs?'
And the dead sailor replied, 'No God, captain.
It was my one job to chart a course by the stars
but during a sudden squall the tiller sheared off,
fell away behind with me hanging on.
And even half-drowned I cared less for myself
than I did for the vessel and those still sailing on,
adrift in the dark without helmsman or helm,
in the heaving ocean, through valleys of waves.

For three nights in weather out of the south
I was swept along by currents and gale-force winds,
then next dawn, pitched high by the swell,
I caught a glimpse of Italy's jagged peaks.
I swam stroke by stroke, trod water, swam again
till I felt shingle underfoot, sand between my toes.
But sheer cliffs and savage rocks defeated me;
in heavy waterlogged clothes I hung on by my nails
till cold and weakness prised my fingers from the stone.

The tide owns me now. Where day-glo life vests
lie beached and disembodied at first light
I roll in the white surf at the water's edge.
Comrade, throw soil over my washed-out flesh
or offer your hand and pull my body aboard,
land me where I can rest in peace in the earth.'

The Wishing Hole

Exit the known world.
Hang a right off the red gravel track,
enter the curtained wood
where muted evergreens part.
Trust to a path underfelted
with dead needles and moulted fir. Follow
the narrow fairway of sky,
hurdle or limbo each fallen trunk,
pass through chambers where timbers lean
like abandoned lances or longship oars –
the old campaign. Then switch left.

Here is a spot: an opened tomb, a roofless dome.
Note the lawned bank, the tropical ferns, remember
that stump of rock – somewhere to sit –
and the tea-coloured moonshine poured from
            a high spout
bearded by bracken and mist, here
where the mammoth sank into stone,
where the bear stashed its cubs,
where the wolf diluted its blood.
Ink well. Cloister. Temple. Pot.
In fact you have stumbled on something
you buried once under a trapdoor of turf
and carpeted over with moss, then forgot.
In fact you have lifted the lid

on your own still – elicit, remote –
where your own ideas percolate
into the barreled calmness, into the mind's cask.
Every thought in your head – this is the source.

Watch a silver coin flicker its way to the pool's depths.
Or hold out both hands with interlocked thumbs,
conjure the moment, let fly a dove.

November, 1962

Even in high summer the old news hasn't thawed:
the white hell of the blizzard,
the mortician's colourless sheet
drawn over valleys and peaks,
the tractor turned-turtle down in the ditch,
one sock, worn as a mitten, discovered
handless and stiff,
lacewood crooks probing fathomless depths,
the two shepherds – found
within shouting distance of house and hearth –
asleep forever under the snow's fleece.

Beyond those deaths,
beyond where the bulldozer spun in its tracks,
a party pushed on, waded and shovelled
through head-high drifts to arrive at a door
with a heavy sack of provisions and grief,
bereavement's inedible loaf,

condolence and sympathy offered
like lamp oil and lint.

Even decades on
stands of pine
keep vigil on neighbouring moors,
snow-poles marshal footpaths and drove roads across the hill,
the snuffed lanterns of old thistles mark the approach.
Next to the stone cairn
this poem hangs its invisible wreath
on the breeze.

Holywell Cottage and Black Pool

Like a long train of daughters and sons
from hamlets and lone farms
way back in the moors and hills
the burn has paraded this far,
come spilling and skidding
through narrow channels and chutes,
tripped headlong over big-dipping linns and brinks,
a procession now of uncountable couples linking arms,
its surface creamy with hems and frills, sunlight
panning for seeds of gold-rush gold in its depths,
the whole carnival rolling
giddy and gossipy
into the grand staircase under the bridge.

Where it slows. Where it pools.

Above the earth veranda
the tumbledown dwelling,
mothballed in lichen and thick grass,
the brazier cooled to a pale orchid,
the manger swaddled in moss.
Outside, three spruce trees attend,
bearing resinous baubles as gifts.
If it snows or a robin bobs on the broken wall
it's a Christmas card, never mind
that the wild holly behind the gable end
stands spiked and beaded with red.

Then it's over the lip
and into the next flume or bend.
There's a wedding downstream, and from here to the church
the burn is a living river
of stags and hens.

Hey Presto

Ladies and gentlemen of the washed-out riverbank I give you
a kingfisher:
the sheet lightning the hairline crack the festival flypast
of a kingfisher;
the afterglow of an arc welding torch under closed eyelids
of a kingfisher;
the flash of turquoise satin under a sackcloth dress the flash
of a gangland tattoo under a starched white cuff
of a kingfisher;

the stray electron the Higgs boson the static spark
of a kingfisher;
the unrepeatable telepathic thought
of a kingfisher;
the vapour trail of an aquamarine-and-amber-tasselled
tranquilliser dart
of a kingfisher;
the single amp discharged from aluminium foil
into the molar root
through a gold crown
of a kingfisher;
the well-timed expletive the sniper round the split atom
of a kingfisher;
the Logan Sapphire knocked overboard from the stern
of the oligarch's rosewood yacht by the teen bride
of a kingfisher;
the first one trillionth of a millisecond after the Big Bang
of a kingfisher;
the déjà vous
of a kingfisher;
the déjà vous
of a kingfisher;
the sonic boom without the sonic boom
of a kingfisher;
the lassoing azure light of the speeding ambulance reflected
in the blank windows of the charity shops on the esplanade
of a kingfisher;
the noiseless shadow of the first Maglev train of the morning
through a Shanghai suburb
of a kingfisher;

the tracer bullet the shooting star the Doppler effect
of a kingfisher;
the missed heartbeat the dropped stitch the kingfisher-like
kingfisher

of a kingfisher.

A Proposal

Wind out of the southwest
scalps the ridge,
careens up the ramped spine of the hill
then over the ramparts between cairns.
Even on good days
the strewn boulders
are pierced with toothache, groundwater
slobs in the jellied peat, the common sundew
digests its antipasto of spider and fly,
and impish dwergen
with glow-worm lanterns
usher the unsuspecting and lost
towards sink-holes and crags.

So it's not without risk we've climbed
the rickety ladder of Simonside, hauled out
onto its vaulted roof,
the cavernous nave echoing underfoot,
and followed the paved aisle
fringed with cloudberry tea-lights
and heather bouquets,

to pause here where the view
is a Taj Mahal of empty space.

Stand next to me now on this altar stone,
its threshold just one step from the rest of our lives,
the acres of years to come
rolled out at your feet.
Here's bilberry for your lips,
low cloud for a morning suit,
an emperor moth for a buttonhole,
here's cottongrass for a dress.
Now all of England has gone down on one knee,
listening, hoping you'll say yes.

Homesteads

Somewhere after the last dumb phone box.
Somewhere the pylons won't go – they've plotted
a simpler contour and stepped aside.
The road insolvent beyond here,
the cart track petering out –
you've had to park up and walk.

The map has it mapped but can't describe
the abandonment of abandonment:
the earthwork bones of skeletal farms and fields
lying semi-detached
with the pebble-dashed bungalow left to rot,
its windows pecked out,
its door unhinged by the universe.

As if evolution brought us to here, to this:
the tiled fireplace,
the Bakelite switch, the cast iron range, the bathtub
now a jackdaw's midden,
the outhouse renatured by nettle and shepherd's purse,
the aerial of a rowan tree
wired into the roof by its roots,
one buttercup – its satellite dish.
Bewitched hawthorns stoop through the kitchen garden
picking a harvest of thorns. In the orchard
a single ash, many-fingered, holds out.

Unsettled, the hills have moved on, pitched camp
in the higher hills.
We are tenants only.
Even to fix that in words is to write on the air
with a fallen crow feather dipped in rain.

Di-Di-Dah-Dah-Di-Dit

di-di-di-dit dit di-dah-di-dit dah-dah-dah
di-di-di-dah dit
di-di-dit di-di-di-dit di-dit dah-dah
di-di-di-dit

dit di-dah-di-dit dah-dah-dah
di-di-di-dah dit di-di-dit di-di-di-dit
di-dit dah-dah dah-dit dah-dah-dah dah
di-di-di-dit dit di-dah-di-dit

dah-dah-dah di-di-di-dah
dit di-di-dit di-di-di-dit di-dit
dah-dah di-di-di-dit dit di-dah-di-dit dah-dah-dah
di-di-di-dah dit di-di-dit

di-di-di-dit di-dit dah-dah
dah-dit dah-dah-dah dah

Hence

I have named myself Hence, dumbstruck diviner
of glassy waters, mindful of depth,
naked except for these weathered tidemarks
rising from anklet to garter to belt,
ponderous figurehead churched in this overturned ark
where Cnut and Swithun drowse in their lifeboats –
they'll launch on the next big surge.

Late-human in form I stand plumb-bob straight
at the spine, but my people drew cloudbursts
into the streets and our rivers baubled the trees
with sheep, so I'm hangdog, bowed at the neck,
of the tribe Narcissi whose mirrors have to be wept
into cupped hands. Admire me by all means,
kaleidoscoped here in the soft scalloped light
of the crypt, but know my consequence.
I am *therefore*. *Thus*. Baptise me as Hence.

MANSIONS IN THE SKY — THE RISE AND FALL OF BRANWELL BRONTË

William, It Was Really Nothing

The young pretender has cocked his hat
towards Westmorland. Picture the great bard,
mid-breakfast, letter in hand,
eyes on stalks and jaw hanging loose,
a loaded knife blade of local damson preserve
stalled between lidded porcelain jam pot and toast,
blood-scabs of red sealing wax crumbed
on the cloud-white tablecloth.

(Thinks: if Paul Pogba cost eighty nine million plus,
what am I worth?) Except

what glittered like charmed finches over Haworth Church
drifts as rain across Scafell Pike. No reply:
the parsonage clock patrols the night-shift
in jailors' boots. Outside the moors play dead.

Initiation

It's leap year day
    eighteen-thirty-six
        when we lift the lid

on curtained rooms
    in the Three Graces Lodge
        to witness the scene:

how the novice is drawn
    from antechamber
        to inner sanctum

blindfolded, noosed.
    How his bared right arm
        and bared right leg

wear a downy haze
    of ginger hair.
        How he kneels,

bible in hand,
    knife and compass
        aligned to his breast,

to swear the secret
    of tokens and grips,
        and receives his tools –

the gavel and set-square
    and sinker of lead
        to keep him

centred and level, sober and sane.
    Then he wobbles home
        up the cobbled lane.

Wallet

Man-purse, portion
    of heart, hank
        of man-heart,

the rolled heart-meat
    tethered
        with tongue-strap,

the hide weathered
    by hand-sweat,
        body heat.

Boned fillet
    of man-breast,
        flipped open it's

book-like,
    the heart-steak
        knifed into folds and layers,

the splayed leaves of flesh
    lying tooled
        and grained.

This pocket
    for banknotes, bills,
        this crevice

for love-letters, verse.
    Deeper in,
        a condom pouched

in its tinfoil wrap,
    the looped pencil holder
        holstering

one clean syringe,
    a dealer's number
        encoded, stowed

in a secret tier,
    credit cards
        maxed to the limit

and edged with coke,
    the prile
        of photo-booth snaps,

dead faces interred
    with a sprig of hair,
        clutched in the heart's heart.

Lost and Found

1) LOST

Stolen or unintentionally removed, one artist's daybook and journal, hand-stitched vellum bound in the choicest rhinoceros hide and fastened with white-gold buckle. Of incalculable creative value, said object comprises detailed ethnographic portrait studies, philosophical observations, intellectual meditations, Latin and Greek inscription, archaeological illustrations from the classical period, delicate line-drawings and original drafts of poetic works (including short formal lyrics and extracts from epic cycles) in the modern 'Romantic' style. Artefact immediately identifiable via its quality penmanship, mature quillwork and distinguished calligraphy. Owner an educated gentleman of forgiving heart; finder assured at least a footnote in the annals of British art and literature plus the gratitude of the nation. Reward: declared upon presentation.

2) FOUND

One smallish notebook, unruled paper, dog-eared leaves, much discolouring (some staining). Contents: pencil scribbles, ramblings and doodles to most pages including amateurish cartoon profiles and caricatures, juvenilia, doggerel and shopping lists in a childish hand, plus evidence of train-spotting. Distinct whiff of alehouse. Some bite-marks. Also contains occasional profanities, questionable theological statements and crude anatomical representations (Parish Magistrate duly notified). Recovered

from wasteland near the Lord Nelson Inn, Luddenden
Foot, along with masonic apparatus (see separate listing)
and bloody handkerchief (incinerated upon discovery).
Assumed local owner. No intrinsic worth but of some
personal or sentimental value, possibly. To be held for one
week only.

Self Portrait

Allow me this moment
all to myself. Doctor,

there was no room to breathe
at the family gathering;

thin-skinned and out of kilter
I ducked behind

a thick stone pillar
then slipped outside

to Facebook and vape.
Doc, it was a no-brainer:

airbrush my own face
out of the picture

or photo-bomb
those darling ~~bitches~~ ~~witches~~ sisters

and moon there forever,
the eternal gooseberry.

So here's me having
a moment to myself,

clearing my head
as best I can,

all light and air, also known as
the nothing I am.

The Smallprint

I)

Simultaneously
and with both hands:
that's how well (they said) he could write.

II)

Elf-words, pixie-talk,
the sub-atomic scribble
of imps and sprites.

III)

Popular wisdom decrees
you can't fold a piece of paper
more than seven times.

IV)

At that age, to confuse signature
with autograph
would be a tell-tale sign.

V)

The word Robins-
on takes some spotting
with the naked eye;

VI)

(treasure hunters – it's
column two, just after halfway down,
right hand side).

VII)

The script-work's bacterial,
with antibiotics
still a hundred years down the line.

VIII)

Pinch-points at the corners,
stresses and fraying along the creases
and rhymes.

IX)

The day comes
when every adult must
up their font-size.

X)

Right under his nose,
the reams and sheaves to which
the old man was blind.

XI)

Using the Rorschach test,
read into those watermarks
whatever you like.

XII)

Mostly at the holes now
is where we notice
the light.

Little Henry

This is the story
  of poor Little Henry:
begotten on Thursday,
  beloved on Friday,
bereaved on Saturday,
  believed on Sunday,
beleaguered on Monday,
  besotted on Tuesday,
belittled on Wednesday,
  besmirched on Thursday,
befuddled on Friday,
  bedevilled on Saturday,
becalmed on Sunday.
  Poor Little Henry,
that was his story.

Verdopolis

A deathbed dream:
I've strolled unchallenged
past merchants' houses
to an arched bridge

medieval in structure,
the glazed river sliding away
underneath, behind me
a duomo or domed palazzo:

it ain't Bradford.
The next scene's a tad sketchy
(a moat? portcullis?):
inside the island-château

I've climbed
the spiral timber stairs
of the highest tower
to a lantern-turret

to paint the landscape.
But in that instant
all the words I've ever written
rise and flap

like panicked birds,
choking the sky, and letters
wuther like black snow
in the final blizzard.

The Gos Hawk

(after Thomas Bewick)

This ſplendid creature,
    though thoroughly native,
    is ſeldom ſeen
in our fields and foreſts.

The male of the species
    is smaller but more vicious,
    feeding on mice
and birdlings, plucking and tearing

and swallowing pieces whole
    then later disgorging
    pellets of hair,
fur, feathers and indigestible bones.

In the Far East, such predators
    are authority's symbol
    when flown from the arm
of the Great Emperor's grand falconer,

and a sight to behold, doubtless,
    by those many thousands
    of inferior rank
who are servants and followers.

In olden times
    the custom and practise
    of sporting a hawk
was confined to those persons

of true means and proud definition,
    for a man might be known
    by his hawk
and his horse and also his hound,

though ladies too
      are ſometimes depicted
      with hawks at their wriſts,
bearing their raptors thuſly.

Of high eſtimation, nevertheleſs
      the bird is renowned
      for its indolent traits
and lack of courage, compared

to the Merlin, Hobby or Jer-Falcon,
      its longer-tailed, ſwifter
      and (ſome would ſay)
more coveted, illuſtrious couſins.

The End

So death comes as a death-like figure.
You thought its shape in the long meadow
was a stone gatepost or dwarf elder,
but made the fatal mistake one evening
of catching its eye, staring too deeply.
At which moment it stepped forward.

True, you can outpace it, no problem,
stay miles ahead of its cheese-wire garland,
years in front of the chloroform nosebag.
Also true, you have in your favour
a tongue dripping with liquid silver,
the cute looks of a Celtic Jesus,

spring-heeled boots and that polished sovereign
hooked from your sleeping father's pocket.
But death keeps on stalking, drawn onwards,
not stopped or stalled by gritstone or gable,
till the night comes when your mind's too brittle
to grip and twist the childproof bottle:

downstairs you hear the back door open
and close, footfall in the flagged hallway,
a mock scream from that warped floorboard
outside the bedroom. You roll over
and face the wall, just lie there frozen
watching its scrawny shadow rise and harden.

A Twofold

Through snow like sleep that arrived
as we slept – the wall and the hedge
bandaged with snow –
snow felting the road

where we trod before light
leaving the door unlocked –
no goods to our name –
snow like a barn owl

or maybe a real owl actually swept
from the barn as we went so far
letting the child in us go
but keeping the smudged star

of the porch lamp in sight
to return through featherfall
bearing the lamb – bringing
the child in us home

through snow like sleep that arrived
as we slept – the wall and the hedge
bandaged with snow –
snow felting the road

where we trod before light
leaving the door unlocked –
no goods to our name –
snow like a barn owl

or maybe a real owl actually swept
from the barn as we went so far
letting the child in us go
but keeping the smudged star

of the porch lamp in sight
to return through featherfall
bearing the lamb – bringing
the child in us home.

FLIT

In 2017, disillusioned by the domestic cultural scene and in search of a more depersonalised aesthetic, the poet Simon Armitage relocated to the small mid-European state of Ysp, and more particularly to its eponymous capital city. With no local contacts and only an out-dated pocket dictionary to hand, Armitage rented a small apartment in a former leprosy hospital and spent a year exploring Ysp's medieval backstreets, latter-day shopping malls, housing districts, redeveloped docks and rural hinterlands. As a stranger in a foreign country and with time on his hands, he made frequent use of Ysp's social amenities and public spaces, including its parks, gardens and museums. The poet was also briefly (and unsuccessfully) employed as a night-watchman by a company providing security services for local galleries.

The poems that emerged from this self-imposed exile or 'retreat' represent a humbling and occasionally confusing period in Armitage's life. They also form something of an alternative guidebook, describing Ysp through the eyes of an outsider, blind to familiar landmarks and official attractions.

A handful of the pieces included here are 'translations' from Ysp's most famous poet, HK. Known only by his initials, HK was most likely a Danish immigrant who arrived in Ysp in the 1890s, probably on a sea-barge or trading ship. Over the course of three or four decades he scribbled upwards of two thousand poems in the margins and end-papers of books in Ysp's National Library, some of which are still being discovered today. Written in a combination of Danish, colloquial Yspish and pidgin Latin, all translations of his work are at best approximations. The stone headstone inscribed 'HK' in the central cemetery was erected in 1963; the then mayor claimed it was to honour the poet's reputation though most interpreted the gesture as a cynical ploy to attract tourists. Either way, the 'resting place' is now Ysp's fourth most visited site, even if the absence of any records relating to HK's existence suggest he died penniless and was buried as a pauper in an unmarked grave. A published undergraduate bibliography by the poet Katerina Brac, herself something of an enigma, remains the most reliable and convincing reference work on HK's poetry to this day, though it is sadly out of print.

*

Aubade

Those blurred indigo hours
    at the thin end of night,
        the length of the fluted spire

afloat in the violet lake,
    a purple fox on the hillock
        waiting to catch fire.

HK

Small Hours

They close the station at one a.m., the last train
being the so-called Graveyard Express,
a sleeper service with curtained windows
which pulls out noiselessly, slinking into the east.

Seen through the padlocked iron gates
the one light in the concourse spills from the shrine
of a vending machine stocked with the shiny saints
of chocolate bars and fizzy drinks, which tonight,

for reasons unknown, suddenly spews its profit
of grain-coloured coins into the empty hall.
From its roost in the rafters, a one-legged pigeon
floats down to sample the cruel feast.

The Sommelier

One evening I'd mistaken the golden glow of the Visitors'
Centre in the woods for a public bar and walked in on a
private wine-tasting event. 'Just take a seat,' said the host,
assuming I was one of his clientele and pouring me a glass
of chilled French Viognier. Over the next couple of hours
he talked us through the noble art of wine-tasting and its
associated techniques: how to tip the glass towards the light
and look for the 'halo' or 'horizon' of transparency around
the circumference of the liquid; how to swirl and sniff; how
to let a wine linger on the palate to assess its 'length', and
so on and so forth. 'OK to swallow?' asked the woman in

a royal-blue trouser suit sitting in front of me, noticing the spittoon in the middle of the table. 'Why not, you've paid for it!' said the host, uncorking a near-transparent Gavi di Gavi and moving through the room with the bottle in one hand and a cute little towel over his free arm. All evening he encouraged us to trust to our instincts as we described each wine according to its aromas and flavours, and by the time we got to the Chilean Pinot Gris I'd built up enough confidence to throw out a few suggestions. 'Roses,' I said. 'Good,' he replied. 'Lime, potato,' I ventured after draining a glass of off-dry German Riesling. 'Excellent,' he said. There was a ten-minute 'comfort break' before we embarked on the reds, by which time I'd really got into the swing of it. 'Plums. Tobacco. Chocolate,' I proposed after downing a mid-price Argentinian Malbec. 'Very good,' said our host. A few glasses later, after a ripe and well-balanced Zinfandel and a somewhat indistinct Pinot Noir, I blurted out, 'Rhododendron.' 'OK,' he said, a little warily. 'Bovril. Cement. Old man's slipper,' I shouted. 'You've tasted an old man's slipper?' he came back. 'I have now,' I said, waving a glass of Chianti Classico in his direction. The room exploded with laughter, after which there was no stopping me. Someone had to get the party started, and anyway, who did he think he was – the pope or something? – passing amongst us with the blood of Christ? Other people were joining in now, barking out wild and absurd comments, some of them unsanitary or sexually explicit, and as the hilarity and barracking grew louder the defeated host eventually slipped his arms through the sleeves of his tailored linen jacket, tucked his personalised corkscrew in his breast pocket, stuffed the sheaf of tasting notes into his holdall and exited the room. After which it was just a free-for-all, everyone dispensing with ritual and formality, popping open bottle after bottle and glugging everything and anything straight from the neck, happily oblivious to issues of provenance and domain.

Although Ysp wines have no international reputation to speak of, the country claims a viticulture dating back to the medieval monasteries of the twelfth century, and climate change combined with developments in frost-resistant propagation have accounted for a significant increase in yield over recent decades. I was surprised how much knowledge I'd absorbed that night, and also how quickly I managed to scan the label of a 2015 local red before the bottle crashed against the bridge of my nose, a powerful, full-bodied Grenache/Shiraz blend from one of the newer 'boutique' wineries to the south. Staggering home in the moonlight I'd nipped into the alley behind the loading bay for a pee, and that's when he got me. 'How did that strike you?' he said, blotting a few splashes from his tailored linen jacket with a silk handkerchief. 'I'm getting liquorice, plasma, formaldehyde,' I had time to say, before my knees buckled and unconsciousness pulled its heavy canvas bag over my head.

Art and Craft

This boathouse and boat deep in the forest
were built by God. As a young man
he'd come here most days with a packed lunch
and his grandfather's carpentry tools

but moved on to increasingly complex jobs –
volcanoes, armadillos, the Great Barrier Reef –
and never came back to carve the date-plaque
or even put water in the creek.

A million million years later he's sitting
in purple robes eating his banquet-for-one
when under the last slice of Kobe beef
there they are – the stranded cedar dinghy

and open-sided shed with its shingle roof –
painted in simple Willow Pattern
on the pearlware plate. And he weeps
for the sharp steel chisels in their velvet socks,

for the spirit level's clear unblinking eye
and the hand-cranked drill, for the devout labour
of working with timber and grain.
Somewhere past and future it begins to rain.

The Impressionist

O famous reclining bronze woman
bolted to your concrete mattress
in a field full of lambs' tails and sly rooks;

tourists threw pound coins into my cup
when I mimicked your sideways mouth
and scraped-back hair and your eyes
like sheep droppings squashed on the road
and your housemaid's knees and bent spine.

Then the wind swung abruptly about
and I watched you skipping off to the woods
in your trailing skirt, dandelion clocks
exploding under your silk slippers,
leaving me metal, frozen, mute,
my eyes like half-sucked boiled sweets
spat from the mouth of a spoilt child.

Displacements

Some nights we zigzag
    down to the quay
        to gawp at the super-yachts

moored in the bay overnight,
    chrome and glass assemblies
        with permanent staff

in matching gilets and shorts,
    a cool thousand euros
        per cubic foot, unmoved

by the tipsy slosh
    of the waves.
        But the bigger dream

is the one vessel
    of rosewood and brass,
        some grand old craft

standing high in the water,
       glimpses of chandeliers,
              a wife and daughter

in matching pashminas
       descending bannistered stairs,
              verandas to all three decks

(no touching, though – you'll tarnish
       the mirrored finish,
              the high glaze).

On the dirt track
       walking home from the shore
              there's a roadside shrine

shaped as a small white church
       beaconed with candlelight.
              You can slide your arm

through the open door
       and down the aisle
              till your fingers

are four villagers, women
       huddled around the priest;
              past midnight now,

the horizon drowned
       and the last fishing boat
              still not back from the sea.

The Installation

I've picked up just enough of the native tongue
to read this report in the *Daily Post*.
A cleaner at Ysp's Museum of Modern Art
(thrown out of the matrimonial home,
it doesn't say why – 'incompatibilities' of some sort)
began spending nights in his place of work,
sneaking back after dark, disarming the sensors
then dossing down among great and priceless works.

He was found out and due to be sacked, but
crowds appeared in the evenings hoping to catch a glimpse,
staring through windows, stealing grainy snaps
of the unnamed man, some well-wishers
leaving him food, toiletries, blankets, poems and books.

Now critics have dubbed him 'the living statue',
a spectre in slippers and stripy pyjamas
drifting through half-lit galleries, cocoa in hand,
or camped on his bedroll under a bronze horse.

In the photograph, standing outside in the snow
his daughter has slipped off her woollen mitten
and touches her fingers to his through the wall of glass.

Corvus corone

Local folklore insists
the crow was an anvil once
but grew tired of the blacksmith's fist.

That its colour is pure bruise,
more purple or Prussian blue.

That only its shadow can fly.
That it shits coal, weeps tar.
That it feeds nails to its young.

That it rarely flinches, but rather
wheels slowly away
whenever sword strikes sword
in the afterlife.

That poets should steer clear,
give it a wide berth.

HK

A New Career in a New Town

David Bowie called. Before I could get into the specifics
of him being dead and this being a private, unlisted
number, he said, 'That's a foreign ring-tone, man – are

you abroad? Always had you pegged as a bit of a stop-at-home, curled up in your Yorkshire foxhole.' I told him I was in Ysp, flirting with communism, alienation and Class A narcotics, and working on my experimental Ysp trilogy. He said, 'Simon, your imagination is telling lies in the witness box of your heart. But listen, will you write the lyrics for my next album?' 'Why not,' I replied, and quickly we thrashed out a plan of action. It would all be done by electronic communication – no personal contact, no face-to-face meetings. David *laid down some backing tracks* and over the next year or so I worked up a suite of songs – verse-chorus stuff, nothing too pretentious or avant-garde. 'These are genius, man. You could have been a poet!' he said, laughing like a cheeky cockney in the saloon bar of a south London boozer circa 1969, his voice like cigarette smoke blowing through a pre-loved clarinet. 'One thing I always wanted to tell you, David,' I said. 'When I was about thirteen I was really into table tennis but had no one to play with. It was just me versus the living room wall, on the dining room table. One night I went down to the local youth club, where all the roughnecks used to hang around, and made my way to the top floor where the roughnecks were playing table tennis, lads who'd stolen cars and thrown punches at officers of the law. I was wearing shorts and sweatbands in the style of my favourite Scandinavian table tennis champion of the era whose deceptive looping serve I hoped one day to emulate and whose life I wanted to live. I felt like a kid goat pushed into the tiger enclosure at feeding time, but they ignored me, those roughnecks with their borstal-spot tattoos and broken teeth, just carried on playing, the small hard electron of the ball pinging back and forth across the net like the white dot in that seventies video game.' 'Pong,' said David. 'Exactly,' I said, 'Just carried on smoking and swearing and hammering the ball to and fro under the yellow thatch of the canopied light in the darkened upstairs room. And here's the thing: every time he hit a winner, the roughest of those roughnecks would sing a line from *Sound and Vision*. 'Blue, blue, electric blue, that's the colour of my room,' he'd croon as he crashed a forehand to the far corner of the table, or 'Pale blinds drawn all day,' when he flipped a cheeky backhand top-spinner past his bamboozled opponent. You probably scribbled those words on a coaster in a Berlin cocktail bar or doodled them with eye-liner pencil on a groupie's buttock, but they'd carried all the way to a dingy youth club in a disused mill under a soggy moor, into the mouth of one of those roughnecks, who's probably dead now or serving life.' David sounded pensive on the other end of the phone, perhaps even a little tearful. 'I have to go now,' he said. I could hear the technician checking his seatbelt and oxygen line for the last time, touching up his mascara, lowering his visor. Then the engines started to blast and the countdown began. I wandered down to the big Henry Moore in the park and lay on my back in the crook of its cold bronze curve, watching the skies, waiting for the crematorium of night to open its vast doors and the congregation of stars to take their places and the ceremony to begin.

Mirage

A false alarm.
    It wasn't smoke
        or heat haze

down in the hollow,
    just a hard mirror
        of standing water

in which
    the sky blistered,
        clouds burned.

HK

Birdlife

There's a sacred heronry now
on the lake-isle
where they hanged traitors back in the day
then left the bodies to rot.

In the glass wall of an office block
on the far bank
suited accountants roost and nest
in the mulberry trees,

each storeyed bough and branch
its own department.
Herons rise from behind desks
to get coffee or lunch,

or flounce from brain-storming sessions
and boardroom spats –
arms flapping, papers everywhere –
heading straight for the ledge.

The Manor

What a prize prick he's made of himself,
trudging a dozen furlongs across the plain

to the widowed heiress's country estate
just to be turned away at the lodge, to stare

from the wrong side of the locked gates.
The plan – admit it – was to worm his way in:

to start as a lowly gofer and drudge, then rise
from gardener to footman to keeper of hawks –

her hooded merlin steady on his wrist –
to suddenly making his way upstairs after dark,

now soaping her breasts in the roll-top bath
with its clawed gold feet, now laying a trail

of soft fruit from her pillow to his, his tongue
now coaxing the shy nasturtium flower of love.

Here he is in the dream, gilt-framed, a gent
in her late husband's best brown suit,

the loyal Schnauzer gazing up at his eyes.
And here's the true him tramping the verge,

frayed collar and cuffs, brambles for hair,
the toes of his boots mouthing like grounded fish.

A pride of lions roams the walled parkland
between this dogsbody life and the next.

Cheers

Legend has it that during the *Summer of Dust*
condensation was the only drink,
and at dawn mothers were seen in the park
collecting dew from tulip petals and juniper leaves
with thimbles and razor blades.

Baptisms were outlawed that year
and only the youngest able to cry.
Radek, a former Royal Palace sentry
and last survivor from Ysp's great drought,
remembers rumours of a marble bath

in a secret room in the cathedral roof
where the archbishop was said to wallow and steam

in holy water syphoned from the font
while his people lowered buckets into the drains.
But he shrugs: 'A city must wash its face,

even when the river sleeps in the mud and bares
the crack of its arse to the skies,' he says.
And the river here is both monster and god:
curse it for its drownings and floods
and the stench it carries from farms upstream,

but to pee or even spit from the bridge
meant a week in the stocks, the stocks
now encased in glass in *Poseidon's* cellar bar
which boasts a liqueur from every nation on earth
and whose signature cocktail is a *glass of rain.*

Apple Cemetery

for James Crowden

Charles Ross,
hammered on Calvados, broke his neck.

James Grieve,
whose blossom allergy was discovered too late.

Lady Henniker,
while dozing in an orchard favoured by vipers.

Laxton Fortune,
drowned in a vat of cloudy cider.

Warners King,
slipped out of a tree.

Annie Elizabeth,
choked on a pip.

D'Arcy Spice,
shot by a rival pomologist in a duel.

Worcester Pearmain,
felled by a second helping of strudel.

The Depths

I asked the lone angler
what species of fish he was hoping to hook.

The common roach with its scarlet trim,
silver-blue armour and bloodshot eyes?
The stately carp in its golden body stocking,
wearing its emperor's moustache?
The fidgety dace, the miserable chub,
the wingless parrot of the fancy perch?
Or maybe the nuclear sub of the pike,
nosing through slimy reeds, its undershot smile
housing a rack of talons for teeth?

But he kept a poacher's silence, statuesque
on the grass bank, his shadow
a tall thin keyhole in the river's skin,

so the pink plastic float
nodded and bobbed in his head, and the line sank
through his throat, chest, stomach, groin,
into the Ganges, Congo, Loire, Orinoco, Blue Nile.

Untitled Fragment:
'Beyond the funeral procession'

Beyond the funeral procession
　　the hot air balloon
　　　　bears fruit.

Beyond the carnival
　　the peregrine
　　　　stoops.

HK

Émigré

I was a child of the fells and hills,
traipsed about on bald naked moors
where even a stunted hawthorn
or wooden fencepost was BIG NEWS.

So I expect marvellous things of these woods:
a venerable hornbeam hung with shoes;
a string quartet asleep and cobwebbed,
ivy wefting through the cello's nerves;

a lamppost in a clearing of pines, its glow
the underwater torchlight in a sea-cave
of luminous bugs and feathered weeds;
the great sudden galleon of a moose.

Behind me, leaves are notelets passed
from tree to tree through infinite dark,
each new poem never anything less
than a written plea for the next.

The Quick Brown Fox Jumps Over The Lazy Dog

Ever since my self-imposed exile began I've been a
regular visitor to a website called *Less Than 100 Grams*.
Dedicated to collectable ephemera of a throwaway
nature and presented in the style of an old magazine
or periodical, its twelve published issues thus far showcase
bottle tops, vintage erasers, model animals (including
a grumpy-looking rhinoceros and a plastic cow), old
postage stamps, toothbrushes, guitar picks (what I would
have called plectrums), neckties, antique bookmarks,
matchbox labels, Polaroid photographs and airline
luggage tags. Issue thirteen features deformed plastic
soldiers in the shape of letters, manipulated and arranged
so as to spell out the phrase The Quick Brown Fox Jumps

Over The Lazy Dog, but the page appears only partially
constructed, leaving the impression that the creator of
Less Than 100 Grams has become disheartened at the lack
of interest in the world of miniatures and abandoned the
whole project to go in search of a big money contract
with a multinational corporation within an expanding
economy. Or has eloped with a giant. In response, I've
found myself making my own *Less Than 100 Grams* list,
which as of this evening goes something like this: banknotes
of the world, dead leaves, earrings, beermats, fingerprints,
apostle teaspoons, butterflies of the Algarve, one night
stands, sunglasses, grass-smoke, déja-vu, Yuri Gagarin
in zero-gravity, an hour in a waiting room, echoes, boiled
sweets of the seventies, fishing stories, house keys, angel
turds, teeth, naked flames, kestrel feathers, pencil shavings,
an estimation of my own worth as expressed in terms
of metric weight, owl pellets, lipsticks, paper cuts, clouds.

The Invigilator

A quiet night in the square,
taxis parked with their sidelights on
and engines cut, drivers muttering
under a fuzzy streetlamp.
A stray dog considers an old milk carton.

Some Guevara type
comes out of the station shouting
'Smash the system',
then staggers across to the Railway Tavern.

I put the binoculars down,
take off the headphones and open the logbook;
it's vital work but written in code,
so to the untrained eye
just hieroglyphics, gobbledygook.

In his town hall office
the deputy mayor boots up his laptop
and unzips his trousers. Painstakingly
a pregnant cleaner extracts
a five pound note from the charity box
with a pair of tweezers.

Dead or Alive

The homeless, starless sky
has come to the window again
begging for crumbs and coins.

Out on the river a goose
barks at the night. A car
clears its throat in the lane.

When I turn out the lamp
the full moon stares through the glass,
five billion years old

and showing its age: pale cheeks;
chin stippled with asteroid strikes;
dead grey lakes

under its cratered eyes.
No wait, it's a wanted poster
plastered with my face.

The Enemy's Song[*]

Our sons were throwbacks and runts, weaklings
who should've been drowned in a bucket at birth.
So say the fathers of those who marched to the east,
so say the fathers of Ysp.

They were bastards and freaks, embarrassing spawn
from drunken one-night stands with donkeys and pigs.
So say the mothers of those who marched to the east,
so say the mothers of Ysp.

They were droopers and dribblers and danglers,
wilting bananas and one minute wonders at most.
So say the wives of those who marched to the east,
so say the widows of Ysp

We flushed our brothers downstream like turds
then opened the windows to let out the stink.

---

[*] A version of this song was allegedly chorused by the soldiers of Chall
towards Ysp forces on the night before the famous battle between the two
countries. If it was designed to undermine morale the gesture seriously
backfired; Yspians overran their eastern enemies in a matter of hours despite
inferior weaponry and an army less than a third in size, many of whom were
irregulars and volunteers. Supporters of Chall's national football club have
recently taken to singing the song at fixtures between the two rival teams,
with a similar lack of success.

So say the sisters of those who marched to the east,
so say the sisters of Ysp.

After the war we changed our names, doctored
their photos with crayons and razors and bleach.
So say the children of those who marched to the east,
so say the orphans of Ysp.

It's dark in the soil, dark where maggots lay eggs
in our hollow bones and our empty veins.
So say the ghosts of the men who died in the east,
so say the dead men of Ysp.

The Lodger

Subletting the spare room to Heidi, the struggling sculptor,
was a big mistake. Soon the beams in the kitchen
bowed under the strain of some massive marble block
and the chisel pecked away at my skull all night.

She kept herself to herself, paid her peppercorn rent
through a crack in the door, left hairs in the sink.
'This can't go on,' I said as we passed on the stairs.
She closed her eyes when she spoke: 'But he's almost
                done.'

A few days later the hammering stopped. Then came
the giggles, the gurgling laughter, the creaking bedsprings
even on Sunday afternoons, then the raised voices
followed by broken plates and cups, then the single shot.

Mozart's Starling

A stray brown dog walked into the gallery
under the nose of the new security guard
who was playing *Assassin's Creed* on his phone.
From here the poem might make one of two moves:
either the mutt goes padding room to room
indifferent to humanity's tortured soul,
sniffing out sweet wrappers and flapjack crumbs,
even cocking its leg against Tony Cragg's *Scribe*;
or it stands awestruck, Tony Cragg's *Skull*
reflected in the shiny buttons of its eyes, and thus
questions of animal consciousness are raised.

But reader, can I hand over the responsibility to you?
This morning I'm bored shitless by poetry;
it's a temperate Bank Holiday weekend
and I'm heading down to the garden hammock
with my iPod and a pack of craft beers from the fridge.
I'll leave a quill and parchment by the desk,
but don't dawdle: in a few minutes' time
that security guard – he's called Frank or Franz –
will turn out the master-switch and go home.

On an Overgrown Path

The alternative guidebook leads
to a partially cleared space in the forest,
but the next page has been ripped out.

What is it I'm supposed to be looking for here?
A flint arrowhead lodged
in the trunk of an ancient oak?
The spot where Janáček sat and composed?
Is this the furthest point from the coast?

Sometimes I go upstairs
then can't remember why.
And when did these flower arranger's hands
at the ends of my arms
become mine?

But I like this place, where a blimp crash-landed,
where ley lines cross,
where a trapdoor leads to an underground church
hewn from a seam of coal, where the sterling silver shoes
from a lost team of sacred horses
are still occasionally unearthed.

Hatches, Matches and Dispatches

A small bronze bell in the gallery roof
is somehow wired
to the city's state-of-the-art maternity suite;
forged from recycled medals

each strike signals a birth,
and visitors coo and cluck
or pull handkerchiefs out of their bags
at the kiss of metal on metal.

A double chime indicates twins,
and the day the bell pealed for quintuplets
even Karl, the hard-nosed maintenance man,
got to his feet to applaud.

Also, whenever brides and grooms
tie the knot downtown
a light snow of confetti
falls from the gallery's eaves,

and a flake plucked from the air
promises good luck. However,
a quick dimming of lights
confirms a new guest has arrived

in the city morgue, upon which
a respectful hush sets in
then dissolves. The tourists roll up,
but such jingling and sprinkling and blinking

disturbs the resident poet,
stalking the halls with his special pen,
attempting to scribble
his little ditties of life and love and death.

Espalier

I feel for that tortured apple tree,
manacled by neck and wrists
to the walled garden's red-brick wall.
Tired scarecrow of broken will,
its existence prised open from birth,
its splayed soul a forced surrender
facing the sun's inquisition all season
till it betrays its people, spills
its secrets, gives up its young.

'Don't fall for it,' said a passing fox.
'Don't blub for the crucified pain
and agonised form because really
it's sunbathing, wearing a blossom wig,
dressed in a choker and bracelets,
flaunting its double-jointed limbs
and vulgar fruits. On full moons
it slips its shackles and dances nude
with the wrinkled old oak.'

Peacetime

No one really believes those police barracks
are student dorms. Through shuttered windows
late night dog-walkers on the path through the woods
have glimpsed truncheons and braided caps
hanging on bedposts and bedroom doors,

or heard raucous gypsy-bashing songs
ricocheting among sycamores.

The constables here carry revolvers
but buy their own bullets;
low wages keep the body-count down,
though like any city
with a history worth knowing the capital boasts
gunshot holes plugged with chewing gum
at chest-height on the cathedral walls.

Overheard in the Aquarium

'He did
a poached haddock
thingummy,

which I thought
on a first date
was pretty sleazy.'

Reliquary

After the Friday market on the wharf,
dark-eyed peasant women from the east
go down on their hands and knees

with knitting needles and bird-bill pliers,
gleaning the quayside, flossing between cobbles

for dropped coins, lost keys and the like.
Whatever they winkle out that isn't currency
they sell as trinkets and charms,
spread them out on colourful headscarves and shawls
along pavements and walls.

A rough translation: 'Things that fell
from the pockets of Christ.' Meaning hairpins,
buttons, a plastic spoon, a baby's tooth,
even ring-pulls from cans of Fanta, offered
as wedding bands or knuckle dusters.

Self Portrait as a Wanted Man

In every new country
he buys new shoes, shells out
the toy money of foreign currency
and wears them *there and then*,
leaves the old pair
standing in the shop
or lays them to rest

shrouded in tissue paper
in the box, or slides them
behind hotel wardrobes,
or casts them off in a lake,

or sets them down before dawn
on the steps of a church
like abandoned twins.

Then he's off down the street
giving police informers the slip,
quick feet planting false tracks,
swerving ginnel to ginnel
in fresh brakes and tyres,
tip-toeing along balcony ledges
and telephone wires.

Then

There was a queue so I joined it.
'To what end?' I asked the haberdasher in front.
'Not the foggiest, squire,' he said, 'But it's long
and it's slow. All the way to the Foundry Gates
and over the hill. It could take weeks.'

He wasn't wrong. In a month
we moved no more than a couple of yards.
But we sang songs, played Cat's Cradle,
Queenie Queenie and Blind Man's Buff,
and a caraway biscuit each was enough.

A girl with one arm piped a tune
on a flageolet made from badger's rib,
and the bloke in the calico britches

folded a hymn-sheet into the shape of a hen,
which laid an egg in his palm.

Memory, obedient friend, dutiful right-hand man,
link arms and skate with me over the frozen dam.

HK

The Dark Stairs

Each blind step
a railway sleeper
quarried from coal,
fossilised treads
marinated in tar,
charred planks
dug out of a fire.
To me they're saying
heaven or hell
it's all the same,
a minor scale
of sharps and flats,
black keys only
this way or that.

HK

Dämmerung

In later life
    I retired from poetry,
        ploughed the profits

into a family restaurant
    in the town of Holzminden
        in Lower Saxony.

It was small and traditional:
    dark wood panelling,
        deer antlers,

linen tablecloths and red candles,
    one beer tap on the bar
        and a dish of the day,

usually Bauernschnitzel.
    Weekends were busy,
        pensioners wanting

the set meal,
    though year on year
        takings were falling.

Some nights the old gang came in –
    Jackie, Max, Lavinia,
        Mike not looking at all himself.

I'd close the kitchen,
    hang up my striped apron,
        pull a bottle of peach schnapps

from the top shelf and say,
    'Mind if I join you?'
        'Are we dead yet?'

someone would ask.
    Then with a plastic toothpick
        I'd draw blood

from my little finger
    to prove we were still
        among the living.

From the veranda
    we'd breathe new scents
        from the perfume distillery

over the river,
    or watch the skyline
        for the nuclear twilight.

Untitled Fragment:
'Evening arrives, then night:'

Evening arrives,
    then night:
        an old Clydesdale

drawing a working narrowboat
    stops to nibble
        on rosehip and catmint

on the canal bank.
    The pipe-smoking bargee
        reckons here

is as good as anywhere else
    to tie up,
        and ties up.

HK

Close Season

Winter arrived this morning.
She'd flown overnight
and was tired and tetchy,
throwing her bags in the boot
and trapping her coat in the car door,
a full-length snow leopard fur
which she cheerfully told me
was *not fake*.

For a woman of such stark glamour
and minimalistic chic
she takes up a lot of space;
already she's claimed the box room
and several empty drawers.
She's painted the windows grey
and stands behind me, unnervingly,
if I pick up a book.

When she goes outside
to shrink-wrap the garden
and lock up the pond
I open her wardrobe,
press a cold white linen blouse
to my face, daren't even caress
the silk camisole top
stitched only by frost.

She has switched the cherry tree off.
The silvery-blue negligee
she draped on the bed
is just breath.

Visiting Katerina Brac

Not a private room
but a quiet screened-off corner of the ward
with its own lamp
and a low window facing the southern hills.
The trolley-bed
like an old sack-truck laid on its back,
the sheets
stamped and tagged, straitjacket stiff
and bread-white,
the pillow dimpled, like somewhere a duck
had slept.
The reek from the kitchen was boiled elk.
The nurse said,
'Yes you look but photograph not allowed.'

I noted
the velvet slippers under the washstand
like dead moles,
a yellowed carton of *f6 Filterzigaretten*,
a ladybird brooch,
prescription sunglasses (four identical pairs),
the folded nightie,
the spent pistil of dried mascara stick,
and a pencil stub
which I'm ashamed to say I pocketed.
In a tall vase
a single lily was far too mortified to speak.

White Page

You're not the angel people think you are,
no holy innocent or uncorrupted child.
Twice or maybe three times a week
you're waiting down some back alley

with your little gang of bullies,
the blank canvas, the uncut stone.
'Come on, hit me why don't you, give it
your best shot,' you keep yelling

before rubbing my nose in the dirt,
grinding my hand under your heel.
Then the boots come in, and once
the splash of warm urine on my back.

The police couldn't care less, yawning,
flipping through books of suspects,
saying, 'Him? Him? How about him?',
every mugshot wearing the same empty smirk.

Last

God for a fortnight, pharaoh
till the generator blows, then what?
This week's most missed:
the shipping forecast; showing off.
Write ALIVE in the meadow
with empty blue oil drums in case
clouds can read/stars give a toss.
Two million years of shame
takes some shucking off – I still
nip behind a wall to exude.

Mandrake prospers in the cracks.
Corned beef and cling peaches again;
note to self: start growing stuff.
Along the station's oxidised tracks
every minute pulls in on time.
Ripples on the lake: ditto, ditto.
On the plus side my golf swing's
unrecognisable these days. Love is:
an afternoon in the glyptotheque
with Madam Kalashnikov.

Nocturne

    The day has counted
   its last grain of corn
into the stone jar.

    A rabbit rusts by the fence.
   Night's umbrella goes up,
moth-eaten by stars.

HK

The Handshake

Spied through a soggy sheep's-wool November mist
the two duellists looked to be standing too close.
'Touching distance' a poet wrote in his book,
his head periscoping over the flooded trench.

Bets were placed on who'd be the first to blink.
Then one man released an unholstered mitt
from his wrist, which flapped into the breach
and hovered there, prompting the other's unfurled fist

to swim slowly forward out of his dark sleeve.
Another poet, standing on piled sandbags
of dead friends, swore he'd seen them meet and mate –
the rude pink bird and the raw pink fish.

Hard to say, though, scanning through shattered glass
across commons drifting with flags and saints.

The Brink

Trawl.
A trawl through the stations:
Florence, Sofia, Luxembourg, Rennes,
Limoges, Malmo, Rome, Budapest,
Riga, Hilversum, Vatican, Lille,
Toulouse, Munich, Helsinki, Prague . . .

St Pancras
Stratford
Ebbsfleet
Ashford
Folkestone
Dover
Sandwich
Ramsgate
Deal . . . on the tuning dial
be your own needle today.
Eavesdrop whatever you can.

Used papers littering the train: headline: *Brits Beat Germans to Sunbeds*. You can reserve a lounger online now, enjoy the Full English buffet at a civilised hour then saunter poolside in hotel slippers and dressing gown, first drink of the day in your fist, tabloid under your arm, no sweat.

Image: deck chair draped with Union flag.

It's a Southeastern stopping service to Englandshire.
You're keeping your baggage with you at all times.

You're keeping what belongs to you by your side throughout.
If you see something suspicious –
see it, say it, sorted – you're going to tell a member of staff.

When out of the tunnel comes Kent:

Cuffed by Siberian snowstorms now and again – Kent.
Kent – dipping its toe in the brine.
Showing a clean pair of heels to the east – Kent.
Kent – garden of England, England's exhaust pipe.
Kent baring its broken white gnashers, growling at Gaul.
Famous British orthodontia showing its all.

Good old Kent, good old the Old Kent Road,
first square on the board.
You were always the Rocking Horse, weren't you,
or was it the Top Hat?

Watling Street thumbing a lift alongside the track:
barefooted wolf-skinned Ancient Britons
            on reconditioned Lambrettas
scootering this way and that.

A Roman Legion parked on the hard shoulder
            in eighteen-wheelers
on the M20, Operation Stack.

Sozzled squaddies trudging home from Agincourt.

Chaucer's ramblers refuelling in Krispy Kreme
at Maidstone Roadchef – first two hours parking for free.

The Home Guard in Jones' butcher's van, manoeuvring.
'Now listen here, Mainwaring.'

Used papers littering the train. Small ads: for sale: antique
radiogram. Requires updated selenium rectifier but other-
wise new. Brass edgings, solid chassis, illuminated display,
golden chain-mail speaker guard, treacly walnut finish –
see your face in the polished grain; cabinet, legs, made in
the days when things were actually things, right? Knobs
that turn. Buttons that clunk into place.

Region, city, frequency, range. Wave:
Hello!
Bonjour!
Hej!
Guten Morgen!
Buna!
Olah!
Część!
Ahoj!

Dia dhuit!: the top of the morning to you, sir,
and the rest of the day to yourself.

Tuning in. Tuning out.

Kent – French-kissing French soil but not quite.
Kent – the hand of friendship amputated at the wrist.
A case of the camel's nose under the tent – Kent.
Phantom limb where there was once connecting flesh.

Overheard: 'I like Europe more when it's over there.'

Overheard: 'Remember when you could smuggle a flick-knife
        home inside a baguette.'

After the city the marshes, after the marshes the downs,
and after the downs the dunes, the shore.

And at Westenhanger a person gets on, a person gets off.

All morning you've been thinking philosophical thoughts,
you've had Erasmus of Rotterdam speaking his mind
        in your mind.
Søren Kierkegaard pecking your swede.
Emanuel Swedenborg taking the stand.
Jaan Kaplinski having his say.
Isaiah Berlin making his case.
Immanuel Kant . . . in Kent!
Niccolo Machiavelli twanging your anvil and stirrup.
Plato's tongue in your head.
You've got René Descartes chipping in
whether you know it or like it or not. Voices, chatter,
they reckon French mobile networks sometimes bleed this far,
bend on the wind, bulge in certain barometric conditions, bow
into OUR AIR.

Folkstone B&Bs like lines of breakwaters
stemming the oncoming tide. Groynes?
It's early though, Folkestone not open yet. Where are
        the Folks?
Chairs on café tables, frightened of spiders and mice,
the first staff of the morning sweeping hardwood floors
with soft brushes, tipping
yesterday into the bin.

You'd wanted a greasy spoon to set you up for the day.
Still, signs of life
in the Zombie Monkey Tattoo Parlour,
people up and doing in the Squidink Tattoo
        and Piercing Studio
by the station ramp: while-u-wait
you could get a nifty St George's Cross
on the back of your neck, or twelve snazzy yellow stars
on an azure square over your heart,
if you were that sort. Be brazen. Go on, pluck up
the bare-faced cheek to brand yourself,
barcode your bare arse.

Field note: model yachts in upstairs windows: nation of sailors.
Field note: this cobbled street, home to alternative art
        and vintage clothes
is the quick way to the front.
Field note: the beach here mainly pebbles and awkward stones.

Big bunches of breeze grabbing armfuls of dead leaves
like ten pound notes.
House sparrows shaken from dreadlocked palm trees
by gusts with stranglers' mitts.

On the Road of Remembrance (actual name)
        hand-knitted poppies
are threaded through black railings, between which
        you can witness
steel-coloured waves martyr themselves on the coast.
The poet's journal illegible at this point,
Moleskine notebook and finest brown ink
blotted and blistered by tears.
Ah, it's the salt off of the ocean what smarts the eyes, you sees.

'The Channel as semi-conductor,' you think it says.

Open skies latticed with autobahns of vapour trails,
the new drove roads,
the new toll roads,
budget airlines laying out silver turnpikes
and fast lanes
and rights of way.

'Mate, there's a gents on the esplanade, but I wouldn't
        if I were you.'

The front mainly Motability buggies, joggers,
dog-walkers and adversarial squalls.
What did you think you'd find:
oast houses and hop kilns lining the country lanes,
a small chapel made entirely from white shells,
day-trading onion-sellers in hooped jumpers riding their bikes,
bobbies on penny farthings, windmills doing Tai Chi
        in the breeze,
a view all the way to the Alps, the Apennines,
the Massif Central, the Pyrenees?

Take a pew. Buy a teapot of tea. Pick a team
on the basis of cool-sounding Eurozone names alone,
shake the Scrabble bag, see how the vowels and
        consonants fall,
let the tongue roll:

Petr Čech
Dejan Lovren
Timothy Fosu-Mensah
César Azpilicueta

Pierre-Emile Højbjerg
Mesut Özil
N'Golo Kanté
Davide Zappacosta
Marko Arnautović
Marouane Fellaini
Zlatan Ibrahimović

Or during your pain-au-raisin
consider Kent as seen by Caesar from the sea.
Consider us Brits as we looked to him:
lank-haired, clean-shaven except for the upper lip,
bodies smeared blue with woad.
How foreign we are to ourselves, how weird.

Masts and aerials superintending the town from the
            shoulder of hill,
decoding, interpreting, listening in, this is Dover now.
Dover Priory – the name over the door.
A trawl through the dial,
a crawl through the town.

In the grounds of the church,
three bearded sad-faced gents playing cards on a raised
            table-top grave –
can I notice that?

This way to the Great Shaft.
This way to the Miracle Chapel (feel the flint floor under
            your feet)
This way to the Roman Painted House (closed till
            Spring Bank).

This way to the White Cliffs (though cast in this light,
more French Grey I'd suggest).
This way to the Bronze Age Boat.
That way to the Port.

> '. . . ye men of Kent,
> Ye children of a Soil that doth advance
> Her haughty brow against the coast of France,
> Now is the time to prove your hardiment!
> To France be words of invitation sent!'

In the town museum you can marvel
at Bill Stein's black and white trunks
in a glass case, Channel Swimmer extraordinaire.
(Your mum would be saying, 'I hope he's rinsed those out'.)

You can giggle at doll-sized Claudius
riding through Kent on an elephant's rump.

You can goggle at model reindeer and woolly rhino
and mammoth and bison and bear
passing over the land bridge from here to Calais and back
unchecked.

You can wonder as Anglo-Saxons
turn in their Anglo-Saxon graves
under the Buckland Housing Estate and by the way
if you thought Britain was closed just order the catch
        of the day
overlooking the port with the ferries coming and going
like floating blocks of flats, traffic lights at the end of the pier
– green for go, red for stop – as simple as that? –

or dangle your legs at the Tunnel's mouth and witness
the intravenous to-ing and fro-ing of trains
the twenty-four hour transfusion of lorries and cars,
a laundering shore to shore . . .

On the other hand, look, a dredger trawling for mud.
Sea cranes asleep, pendulous hooks dozing
                on long chains.

You can see from a map
the Tunnel departs or arrives under Shakespeare Cliff –
worth a mention, isn't it?

Kent – its megaphone raised to its lips.
Its spur drawing blood from the Channel's flank – Kent.
Kent – exposing its fat little cock to the east.
Kent – where the country looks over the edge,
                waits on the brink.

Is that Europe on the other side?
The Alhambra? La Scala? The Palace of Versailles?
The ghostship Sandettie Light Vessel Automatic on the blink?
No, just a super tanker treading water at low tide.
Just Dungeness B –
workers in tin foil suits
juggling hot atoms in oven gloves,
treading big vats of ripe atoms into megajuice.

Time you moved on.
        Ticket pre-booked.
                The window seat.
Pill boxes either side of the line like empty skulls.

♫ *On Sandwich Flats*
You thought you'd seen
The footprints of
St Augustine
Who ferried Christ
Across the gulf
Who scurried with
A silver cross
Between the golfers
And the golf ♫

Then Ramsgate right where the map said it was –
the Ordnance Survey – in times of continental drift
there's a name you can trust.

Late afternoon in the seafront pavilion,
as spied through fogged up glass,
tea and scones on paper doilies,
Darby and Joan on the sprung floor
doing the Strasbourg A-Go-Go,
the Brussels Shuffle,
the I Should Cocoa,
the The Hague Hustle,
the Maastricht Excuse-Me,
the Not On Your Nelly.
Those lords and ladies are giving it plenty, they're putting
their whole selves in,
their whole selves out,
in out in out shake it all about,
they do the Hokey Cokey and they turn around.
That's what it's all about.

Europe as musical chairs –
grab a seat or stand when the music comes to a halt.
The last waltz.

Then trawl.
Spectrum of noise, dragnet of sound.
This week's composers of the week:
Frédéric Chopin, Maurice Ravel, Jean Sibelius, Plastic
        Bertrand, Johann Sebastian Bach, First Aid Kit,
        Claudio Monteverdi, Kraftwerk, Nouvelle Vague,
        Leoš Janáček, Aphrodite's Child –
listener, collect your complimentary transistor radio
        from the beach,
put the shell to your ear.

Field note: red sand under Ramsgate pier; sand of the desert;
crepuscular sand; red lines; hour glass sand;
red grains in the hand;
time running down.

Sandbags stacked at the side of the café door,
piled in the lobby to keep out the flood,
galvanised gabion cages stuffed with raw boulders
to shore up the shore.
The marina's palaver, its rigmarole and chandlery.
Small boats at low tide squatting in brown mud,
pennant flags on spindle masts
with LEAVE written on, some saying OUT.

Amusements. The slotties. One-arm bandits and Penny Falls,
the sov in your pocket still good up to this point
but not many nautical miles more.

Whither (you'll use the word 'whither' here)
the Little Ships of Dunkirk?
Or Dunkirk as metaphor – bringing ourselves back?

You've ordered a sundowner for one
in the brasserie-bar
on the open palm at the far end of the harbour arm.

You'll look at the menu:
vinho verde
chicken kebab
Hungarian goulash
Serrano Ham
calzone pizza
Edam cheese
Austrian smoked
the Côtes du Rhône
the Rioja Reserva
Belgian waffles
bottled Tyskie
pretzel
schnitzel
the smørrebrød
a smörgåsbord

The turquoise static of kingfishers
arcing from craft to craft in the galleried bay
under the balconied town,
a grand circle of twilit windows,
opera glasses lifted to Georgian and Regency faces,
all eyes on the broken horizon where Britain sheered off.
Put a coin in the clockwork-telescope-thing on the pier –
on a clear day they say you can see Brexit from here.

Last train to Deal. Last train before dawn.
To be garrisoned under a nail-clipping moon.
To be billeted only a stone's throw from the hem of the sea,
waves fizzing and bickering under the prom wall,
the tide making a fingertip search of the strand,
the pier as a prison landing
patrolling the moorings, the dark, the shallows, a shimmer
of petalled lights on the far coast, mirage and mirror.

So what did you come here to find:
A Dickensian town?
A Powellesque rant?
An Elgarian tone?
A Fallstaffian mood?
A Turneresque light?
A Faragian lunch?
A Churchillian view?
Zeus as a white bull
drunk on the fumes
of his saffron breath,
chewing the cud
in a meadow near Walmer
having bucked Europa
into the water?

Drop the blinds.

Then trawl.
A trawl through the dial, a scan through the scale.

Third. Light. London. West.

This is the Home Service.

Cue white noise.

Notes

Sulpicia's Playlist (1996)

A highly impressionistic version of Poem 7 by the Roman elegiac poet Sulpicia (late first century BC). Commissioned by the *Observer* in conjunction with the 1996 Practices of Literary Translation Colloquium at the University of East Anglia, at the instigation of writer and academic Josephine Balmer.

Making a Name (2002)

The first of several projects with Yorkshire Sculpture Park, the poem was commissioned to mark the installation of Gordon Young's *Walk of Art*, a cast iron walkway leading to the entrance of YSP's Visitors' Centre. For a fee, individuals can have their names cut out of the metal path and 'immortalised'. As more names have been introduced, more metal plates have been added to accommodate them, and the walkway is now over a hundred metres in length.

THE NOT DEAD (2007)*

The film *The Not Dead* was commissioned by Channel 4, produced by Century Films and broadcast on Remembrance Sunday 2007. It represents the seventh poetry/film collaboration between myself and director Brian Hill in which we've attempted

---

* Introduction to *The Not Dead*, Pomona Books, 2008.

to challenge the conventions of factual filmmaking, enhance the voices of participating characters and make memorable television. Although all of our films have been 'documentaries', they have each involved some written or dramatised element, ranging from poetic voice-over to full-blown song lyrics. My role in *The Not Dead* was to listen to the statements of its contributors – soldiers, real people with true stories to tell – and turn their experiences into poems.

Around the time the film appeared, a number of newspaper articles asked why no contemporary war poetry was being written. Most of us read the War Poets at school. Some read the poetry of World War II, but for the majority it was the poetry of the Great War. Today, the poets of the trenches (Wilfred Owen, Siegfried Sassoon, Rupert Brooke, Robert Graves, Edward Thomas, Ivor Gurney and others) continue to hold their place within the canon of English literature and the education syllabus, and for good reason. Put crudely, poetry at its best says something about the human condition, often in relation to death, and the poets of WWI were serious writers operating at the very limit of human experience, sending back first-hand literary reports. It's difficult to imagine an equivalent situation ever occurring again, at least in the West. Most of the poets I know would think twice before setting a mousetrap, let alone enlisting for active service, and I don't have the subscription figures in front of me but I'd guess that readership of *Poetry Review* amongst Her Majesty's Armed Forces is pretty low. True, Brian Turner, the American soldier with the creative writing qualification, published a volume of war poetry which goes far beyond the hobbyist poetry that most people write at some time in their lives, especially to express sadness or loss, but he is the exception who proves the rule.

However, literary poets are writing war poetry today, it's just a question of knowing where to look for it, and recognising it when it is found. Warfare has changed and so has poetry. It could be argued, for instance, that in an art form where context is sometimes just as important as content the permanent backdrop of our current military situation makes almost every poem a war poem. In the same way, a single mention of blood-orange sky or even a shooting star might alert the careful reader to the true metaphorical significance of a poem, even if that poem appeared, at first glance, to be about an empty desert at sunset. Warfare has echoed constantly through contemporary Irish poetry. Of the British, James Fenton, Michael Symmons Roberts, David Harsent, Glyn Maxwell, Peter Reading, Andrew Motion and Jo Shapcott to name but a few have all addressed war, sometimes through the long, lingering shadows of previous campaigns. Others have met war head-on, none more directly than Tony Harrison with his Gulf War poems 'Initial Illumination' and 'A Cold Coming'.

The Not Dead was a war film. It was about returning soldiers, and in keeping with the literary tradition, the mode of expression was verse. There were three main participants in the film. Cliff was a veteran of the Malaya Emergency, Eddie served in Bosnia and Rob fought in Basra. Like Owen and Sassoon before them, they all suffered from what has come to be known as Post-Traumatic Stress Disorder, a version of what was previously referred to as shell shock. Along with other soldiers we interviewed for the film, it was appalling to hear how little help these men had received. Many of the younger servicemen had turned to drink and drugs to blot out images of war, and a significant number had attempted suicide.

For some of the men, being in the film meant reliving their worst nightmares; most of the poems I wrote revolved around a key 'flashback' scene, requiring each soldier to revisit the very incident he was desperately hoping to forget. On this point, it is curious to note how conventional psychological help has proved largely ineffective with PTSD. Most therapy involves dealing with issues, then moving on. But for traumatised soldiers, the harrowing images and accompanying feelings persist, in some cases for a lifetime. It's more a case of learning how to live with them. Rob was part of an attack on a bank in which an Iraqi man was shot as he burst through the doors. Rob doesn't say if he fired the fatal round, but in the days that followed, while on patrol, he had to walk across the dead man's 'blood-shadow' on several occasions. Like many servicemen, being a soldier had been Rob's dream from boyhood. To this day he's patriotic, nationalistic even, but the only Albion he'll fight for now is his beloved West Brom. As he says in the film, he was fully prepared for battle, but not prepared at all for coming home. Since absconding, his life has followed an all too familiar pattern of insomnia, alcoholism, drug abuse, homelessness, violence and crime. He feels damaged and helpless, but most of all he feels forgotten or, worse, ignored.

Cliff's feelings of guilt and shame have only increased with age and the pictures in his head are as clear today as they were half a century ago. At 75 he can't talk about the jungle ambush he was involved in without tears rolling down his face, and when it comes to speaking of his fellow soldiers who died in the attack, he can barely get the words out of his mouth. Time, often thought of as the great healer, has not done anything to diminish his sense of grief; Cliff is a man wearied and condemned by memories.

Of all three servicemen, Eddie appeared to have suffered the most, despite the fact he was serving in Bosnia as a UN Peacekeeper, wearing a 'blue lid'. A born soldier, he expected to shoot and be shot at – that's what he was trained for. Instead, he lifted the barrier at the checkpoint to wave through the death squads. A couple of days later he'd be a member of the party that went in to witness the horror and clean up the mess. He describes, at one stage, a pregnant woman tied to a tree, cut open, with her dead, unborn baby hanging from her womb. There are other things he won't describe, he says, because they are worse. After returning home, to try and cure his nerves and overcome his paranoid reaction to loud bangs, he took a revolver into the middle of a field and fired several blank rounds against his head. He also tried to hang himself from a tree.

I wasn't present when the characters in the film read their pieces to camera, but it couldn't have been easy for them. The Army is a MAN'S WORLD. Trained soldiers are not encouraged to open their hearts, and confessing feelings of vulnerability, insecurity and fear on national television constitutes, in my view, a supreme act of bravery. Rob can hardly lift his face to the camera. Cliff seems to be permanently on the point of collapse. Invited to make himself comfortable, Eddie half-demolished the room he was filmed in, kicking at doors and furniture until it looked like the scene of some unspeakable Bosnian massacre. Then he was ready to start. And the last word came not from a man but from the voice of Laura, Eddie's wife. Tracing the scar of a bullet that took away part of her husband's face before pinballing through his body, she describes the slow and painful process of trying to reach him, touch him, love him, and make him human again. In the film, the scene provides an obvious, ironic contrast with Britain itself, its majors and generals bemused, irritated and embarrassed by these broken men, the mother country washing her hands of those soldiers who escaped death only to return home as 'untouchables', or as ghosts.

*

There are nine poems in this book. 'The Black Swans' and 'Scarecrows' were written for Eddie. 'Albion' and 'Remains' were written for Rob. 'Warriors' was written for Scott, a Gulf War veteran who did not appear in the final film. 'The Malaya Emergency' and 'The Parting Shot' were written for Cliff. 'The Manhunt' was written for Laura. The title poem, written to summarise the sentiments of all the returning combatants who participated, was recited in the film by Eddie, Rob and Cliff. Thanks are hereby paid to all those who agreed to take part in this project, and also to Combat Stress, the ex-services mental welfare society, for their advice and support.

PETER AND THE WOLF (2009)

Commissioned by the Southbank Centre to introduce several Christmas screenings of BreakThru Films' stop-frame animation of Prokofiev's 'symphonic fairy tale for children'. The poems were designed as a way of introducing the instruments and their corresponding characters in the story, and formed part of a longer script delivered by an onstage narrator at the Royal Festival Hall, accompanied by the Philharmonia Orchestra.

Advent (2009)

Written for the closing scene of a BBC Four documentary on *Sir Gawain and the Green Knight*. 'Simon Armitage goes on a journey to discover the language and landscape of our first great Arthurian romance, *Sir Gawain and the Green Knight*. For J. R. R. Tolkien, Gawain is "a fairy tale for adults", but Armitage finds strong modern relevance in the trials of its stripling hero and a tale of do or die. A marvel of the imagination, Armitage argues that Gawain must take its place alongside Chaucer and Shakespeare at the head of the canon.' Much as I admire the poem and as often as I have advocated on its behalf, that final claim is one I don't remember making.

Ever Fallen In Love With Someone (You Shouldn't've) (2010)

Published by the *Guardian* as part of a special feature on Glastonbury Festival's fortieth anniversary. Originally and somewhat casually entitled 'Festival', the poem eventually took the name of a Buzzcocks' single to more accurately reflect the event it goes on to describe, which in fact took place at Latitude Festival in Suffolk a few years earlier.

The Watchman's Speech (*c.*2012)

A version of the opening monologue from Aeschylus's *Oresteia*. It had been my intention – and notionally still is – to make a theatrical adaptation of the entire trilogy, but this poeticised piece represents the only progress so far.

Diana and Actaeon (2012)

Part of a project in which the National Gallery invited fourteen contemporary poets to respond to one of three paintings in their Titian exhibition, and published in *Metamorphosis – Poems Inspired by Titian* (National Gallery London, 2012).

WALKING HOME (2012) and WALKING AWAY (2015)[*]

In 2010 I walked the Pennine Way, north to south, troubadour-style, giving poetry readings every evening in exchange for bed, breakfast and a packed lunch. I wrote an account of the journey in a book called *Walking Home*, after which I vowed never to attempt anything as demanding again. Three years later curiosity and restlessness got the better of me; I set off along the north coast of the South West Coast Path heading for the far tip of Cornwall, again as a busking poet, and wrote a book called *Walking Away*. The distances for both walks were remarkably similar – about two hundred and seventy miles – and each journey took just less than a month to complete.

I've always associated walking with poetry, both in the Romantic, Wordsworthian sense of communing with the outdoors, and also on a purely practical level, recognising the walk as a chance for the mind and the body to engage in some

---

[*] Introduction from *Waymarkings*, published privately by Andrew Moorhouse, Rochdale, 2016, with wood engravings by Hilary Paynter.

mutually beneficent wandering. It has been said before that a walk is midway between doing something and doing nothing, a marginal activity that combines contemplation and stimulation, perfect breeding conditions for poetry it would seem. And it's rare that I go out for a walk and don't come back with a poem, or at least the beginnings of one. But in two months of striding down the spine of the northern uplands and along the coast of the south west peninsula I wrote only eight poems, some of them little more than rough notes and speculative scribblings at the time, a pretty poor strike rate given the apparent opportunity. There were a number of reasons, including a tight schedule, the difficulties of writing while walking and thinking while navigating, the (mostly) welcome distraction of fellow walkers, and the fact that I was always conscious of converting experience into prose paragraphs rather than poetic stanzas. I imagined more poems might arrive later, out of memories and with the benefit of hindsight, once the two non-fiction accounts were completed and published. But they never did. I'd moved on.

So eight poems only. And not composed to mark important milestones, famous landmarks or momentous occasions. But significant to me all the same in that they came to represent stolen time, those minutes and hours when I felt able to step outside the itinerary, push the bigger project to one side, and allow myself to daydream. To *dwell* on an idea, in the sense of inhabiting a thought or letting a thought be resident in the mind over a prolonged period. To stay put, somehow, even while pushing forward. Or perhaps the poems could be interpreted as photographs, composed 'stills', compared with the cinematic motion and momentum of the walk itself.

Presented here as a sequence, in geographical and chronological order, I also see them for the first time as 'waymarkings' of some kind, impromptu signposts on an alternative map, less a measure of distance and direction, more like personal attempts to plot a location's mood by cross-referencing it with my own mood on the day. And as far as the two National Trails are concerned, the poems should probably carry the old fashioned warning: 'Not to scale – should not be used for navigational purposes.'

The Lives of the Poets (2012)

Commissioned by The Poetry Society for National Poetry Day.

IN MEMORY OF WATER (2012)*

A full year has passed since the last Stanza Stone was craned into position, and the seasons have done their work. Visiting them recently, I felt as if they were now admitted and accepted forms within the landscape, not natural features of course but as much a part of the Pennine furniture as a wall, marker post or stile. Heather has re-established itself around the two Puddle Stones on Ilkley Moor where a digger had gouged open a resting place for them in the sodden peat; moss and lichen have colonised the letters of the Mist Stone on Nab Hill; in Backstone Beck fluctuating water levels have brought an unexpected palette of green algae and red oxides to the left-hand margins of the Beck poem; the two Dew Stones on Rivock Edge have lost the sheen of newness that initially distinguished the sawn rocks from the ancient dry-stone walls which frame them; the full blast of the weather has calmed and healed the long lines of the Rain poem which, when they were first carved, seemed raw and exposed; and the last time I hiked up the long straight incline of the old truck-track to the top of Pule Hill and turned into the disused quarry, the words of the Snow Stone were inlaid from first capital letter to final full stop with ice, adamantine and almost electrically bright in the winter sun. Seeing it there, reading it, considering how it had become the embodiment of its creative intentions brought an intense feeling of achievement, and for a few self-congratulatory minutes I allowed myself to think of it as the conclusion to a long and very complicated project. I've said on many occasions that if a poem, once written, is exactly the same as its author first imagined it would be, then it is almost certainly a failure, and that artistic success must always involve

---

* Preface to *Stanza Stones*, Enitharmon Press, 2013.

a process of transformation. On that basis alone, the Stanza Stones are a success story for the simple reason that they actually exist, because until that final sun-struck, ice-shining moment I didn't really believe they were possible.

In a cold church hall at the back of Ilkley Literature Festival's terraced office in late 2010, Rachel Feldberg proposed some kind of collaboration or commission, though at that first meeting I don't recall either of us having any firm ideas. Rachel wanted the project to be immediate and participatory yet have a long-term legacy; I'd just walked the Pennine Way and had been struck by the number of markings and carved signs along the route. It was probably the coming together of those ambitions and experiences that led to the notion of poems in the landscape. Or poem singular to begin with, because my original impulse was to identify an abandoned quarry face or hillside and carve huge letters into it, creating a poetic Mount Rushmore somewhere within Yorkshire. I'd worked with Antony Gormley on a couple of projects in the past and was always impressed with the scale of his ambition and the courage of his convictions when it came to situating art out of doors. Like the Great Wall of China, maybe this poem would be one of the few man-made objects on earth said to be visible from the moon . . . In the end funding considerations, reality checks and a few bouts of humility forced us to redefine the parameters of *Stanza Stones* and rethink its aspirations, and all for the better. A new territory came into focus, that of the South Pennine Watershed, the moorland region which by a fluke of convenience happens to extend from my home village of Marsden in the south to Ilkley in the north, and a new endeavour came to mind, that of creating a suite or succession of poems to be sited at intervals across those moors, to be carved into existing or introduced stones. Everything then seemed to fall into place very quickly, from the appointment of a landscape architect and a letter-carver to the procurement of goods, services, permissions and promises, until suddenly the only thing holding back the commencement of a major public art enterprise/construction project was the small matter of half a dozen poems. When would they be ready, and what would they say?

[174]

Animated against the skyline, the Cow and Calf are two weather-sculpted rocks which form part of a longer escarpment of exposed gritstone to the north-facing ridge of Ilkley Moor. In silhouette against the horizon they have taken on an iconic significance for the town of Ilkley itself, and the nearby restaurant, café and car park testify to their popularity among picnickers, climbers, walkers, day-trippers and the like. Although the two stones themselves haven't gone unscathed, graffiti artists armed with knives or chisels have tended to favour neighbouring outcrops; many are scored with names and dates going back as far as the eighteenth century but also bear more recent contributions from courting couples, football fans and admirers of particular rock bands. Thinking of the quarry behind the Cow and Calf as a kind of gateway or portal onto the wider moor, the graffiti can be viewed as a sampler or foretaste of what lies beyond, because for many thousands of years people have been visiting this upland region to offer their prayers and express their desires in the form of carved stones and man-made formations. Ilkley Moor and the encompassing Rombald's Moor have more such monuments than almost anywhere in the western world, from prehistoric cup-and-ring markings, to cryptically decorated and engraved rocks, to enigmatically arranged groups of standing stones. It may seem ironic but it is also of huge significance that sacred or artistic gestures like these should appear in such a high, remote and inaccessible location, appealing for the most part to an audience of nobody, presenting their ideas directly to the gods and the stars above. In many ways, both the inspiration and the permission for the *Stanza Stones* poems comes directly from that tradition, and the poems represent a contribution to an unbroken and ongoing dialogue which has been taking place on the open canvas or blank page of the moors from Neolithic times. Right from the outset I felt the urge to say something both particular and universal, both timely and (immodestly) timeless, and in a style that took its potential readership into account. Because it's one thing to publish poetry in books or journals, to preach to the converted perhaps, but something slightly different to write for a public space or to put poems in front of people who might have no experience of contemporary verse and little interest in it. And different again to compose a poem which might last for a thousand years, whose readers are . . . people from the future. Impossible of course to imagine such an audience or their relationship with poetry of the early twenty-first century, bearing in mind the way language has evolved and transmuted over the preceding millennium. But a thought to conjure with all the same.

Even though I didn't have a subject in mind, my first inclination was to write a sestina, distributing the six stanzas among six different stones. The maths added up – hopefully the language would follow. Those familiar with the sestina form will know that the six end-words of each verse are repeated in a rearranged, pre-arranged pattern, so choosing the right ones is important. But like so often with a poem, the plan had to change. Every time I went to the moor I collected a bit more language until I had several long lists of terms and phrases associated with the territory. I'd choose six and begin writing, but got nowhere. On a couple of occasions I had a vague sense that a poem was beginning to take shape, but it was rarely more than three or four lines, and never that feeling of being onto something. The daydream just wouldn't go on dreaming. The crystal wouldn't coalesce. My poetic teacher, Peter Sansom, once told me that it's sometimes best to forget about a poem for a few weeks rather than struggle or fight with it, to let the subconscious put in its shift. So that's what I did, and when I returned to it with a clearer mind and a clean eye, I saw what the problems were. Firstly I was attempting something formulaic and literary rather than trusting to impulses and intuition. Secondly, the sestina framework seemed too inflexible and stubborn to accommodate the epic geographies and rich vocabulary of the moor. Thirdly, I still had no idea what the poem was trying to articulate. And lastly, I was letting the form dictate the content – a case of the tail wagging the dog, or to use a Yorkshire phrase, putting the cart before the horse. After another visit to the hills, this time in lashing rain, I came back with a different idea and a single purpose. To let water be the overall subject: the water that sculpted the valleys, the water that powered the industries, the water we take for granted. Water – our most vital necessity, our common gold, our shaping force, and our local vintage. And to let the various forms of water provide the topic of each individual and self-contained poem. A piece about rain, a piece about snow, a piece about dew . . . the Rain Stone, The Snow Stone, The Dew Stone . . . and so on. Then a bigger, over-arching title came into my head, *In Memory of Water*. I suppose I saw an opportunity to draw on the often commemorative nature of monumental-masonry and engraving by making an unspoken connection with environmental themes and concerns about climate change. Perhaps I was thinking ahead, pessimistically, to a future where the Stanza Stones still existed but on a planet that had either drowned or boiled dry. It's impossible to say that an idea is 'right'. All I know is that no sooner had the notion occurred to me than the poems started to happen, even to the point where I was anxious to get to my notebook, because words and lines and sentences were queuing up in my head, impatient to be written down. To me this is always the most engaging phase, where the internal, abstract concept of the poem is attempting to materialise externally, where the mind is in negotiation with the world through the medium of language.

It's been exciting to see how others have responded to the same themes in their own writing. Over the course of several months I led groups of young poets up onto those same moors – above Marsden, above Oxenhope, above Ilkley – and gave them no particular instruction other than to collect words. And from those words, firstly through writing exercises in workshops, then later in their own time and space, poems came into being. Some of the group members were already familiar with the Pennine landscape, but others had no experience of it whatsoever, and it was impossible not to grin now and again at the sight of cool city kids in expensive trainers picking their way through peaty bogs, or to see carefully moulded hairdos being blown every-which-way by the raging wind. At the same time it was moving and inspiring to read poems of raw experience, personal insight and genuine feeling, and to see what impression the wild landscape had made on such energetic and unpredictable imaginations.

The Snow Stone, the first to be carved, now forms the beginning of the 47-mile Stanza Stone Trail, a walk that utilises existing footpaths, bridleways, towpaths and other public thoroughfares to connect the poems. Or to 'collect' them, even; I haven't walked the whole trail myself, but those who have seem to task themselves with finding each poem and capturing it in the form of a photograph, and judging by internet sites and blogs the Stanza Stones Trail has already become something of a recognised and established activity. The stones have also acquired their own guardians, walkers mainly, regular visitors who clear a few weeds away once in a while, remove litter from the sites and generally keep an eye on things. Given how exposed and vulnerable I feel the poems to be, I find their informal stewardship greatly reassuring. And also a matter of great pride, inasmuch as people seem to have taken possession of them, even allowed themselves to be possessed by them. Some have written about their favourite stone, and asked me to name mine, and even though it's iniquitous to choose between them I have to admit that having a poem carved not just in the village where I was born but into the side of Pule Hill, a hill which loomed large over Marsden and exerted such a powerful gravity over me as a child, is an extraordinary privilege. I'd go there often, nearly always alone, and I remember finding snow piled up in a corner of the old quarry long after Easter and long after all other traces of winter weather had disappeared. The Snow poem, carved horizontally across two massive slabs that once formed part of a very crude wall or embankment, now strikes me as a sort of poetic Plimsoll line, daring the snow to reach the heights it once did.

The stones could be thought of as sites in their own right, literal landmarks, places to visit. Or they could be thought of as milestones or marker posts along the invisible route of the watershed. A drop of rain falling one inch to the west of the watershed will find its way to the Irish Sea, and one inch to the east to the North Sea; theoretically a person should be able to walk from Marsden to Ilkley along that crest without getting their feet wet, though I doubt this has ever been achieved. And those looking hard enough might stumble across a seventh Stanza Stone, a secret stone left in an unnamed location within the South Pennine water catchment, waiting to be discovered and read.

I want to acknowledge that Stanza Stones was not in any way the work of a single mind, but endlessly collaborative in nature, involving, at the final count, hundreds of helpers, workers and volunteers and thousands of hours of time, much of it given freely and very much appreciated. So despite the name and title of the project, I find myself remembering it not just in terms of stones and stanzas but as a series of human encounters that took place over a two-year period, many of them in astonishing locations and bizarre circumstances. And as a series of conversations ranging from the forensically detailed to the absurdly fantastical, particularly with Rachel Feldberg, director of the Ilkley Literature Festival, who oversaw the enterprise with extraordinary patience and energy from beginning to end, and with landscape architect Tom Lonsdale and with letter carver Pip Hall. I've met very few people who know and respect the Pennine landscape as much as Tom Lonsdale, or have his understanding of its geographies and its processes. Without his sympathetic judgments, professional expertise and common sense not one stone would have found its way into position, and the whole adventure was underpinned by his guidance, his good nature and his optimism. As for Pip Hall of Dentdale, she is a force of nature, and one that did battle with many other forces of nature to see the job finished. Sometimes with her apprentice Wayne Hart but often alone, working by hand and eye, in temperatures that made my fingers feel like they were going to fall off, in blinding rain, in enfolding mists, in pummelling winds, or up to her thighs in the raging torrent of Backstone Beck, she practised a combination of industry and artistry that not only defied the conditions but seemed to draw strength from them. She carved through the wettest year on record, which at one point caused me to wonder if the stones were somehow prophetic or visionary, and made me wish I'd written about sunshine instead, or money. But the heavens brightened every once in a while, and one morning as I walked up onto the moor, the tapping of metal on stone and the sight of her red and white scarf protecting her face and mouth from chippings and dust were the only noise and colour for several miles in any direction. When I reached the rock, the freshly cut letters shone bold and vivid in the early light, full of oranges and yellows and sparkling with minerals. So for a few moments it seemed as if she had opened a chorus of tiny mouths in the stone, each with its own vowel or consonant, and allowed it to speak or sing.

Postscript

On the rainy evening of 14 June 2012, Pip Hall, Tom Lonsdale and myself deposited a seventh, secret stone at an undisclosed location somewhere within the South Pennine watershed. Inscribed with the words 'In Memory of Water' and about the size and shape of a bowling ball, the stone was safely encased within a short, hollowed-out log designed to float, with 'Stanza Stones' carved into the sawn log at both ends.

The location was Lumb Hole Falls in Crimsworth Dean, above Hebden Bridge, and the log was tucked under the bank on the west side of the beck, just downstream of the bridge. Over the next month, and following unprecedented rainfall, the area was hit by a series of floods which not even a royal visit could halt. Houses and businesses in the nearby towns were devastated. A few days after the rain had eased and the clean-up had begun, one of the team made a visit to Crimsworth Dean but the stone had gone, and not surprisingly, given that the deluges and torrents had also carried away trees and boulders. At the point of writing it remains lost, possibly buried in mud somewhere along the Calder Valley, or perhaps floating down the Aire or the Ouse, or maybe bobbing around in the English Channel or further still, having made it through the jaws of the Humber and into open waters.

Zodiac T-Shirt (2013)

American singer-songwriter Beck published *Song Reader* in
2012, an 'album' consisting of twenty songs in sheet music
format. In July 2013 several artists performed the songs
onstage at London's Barbican, and a handful of writers were
also invited along to make appropriate contributions. Given
that *Song Reader* seemed like an exercise in counter-intuition
(i.e. a record that had never been recorded) I attempted to follow
suit with a song-lyric that would never be sung – at least not
by me. With what I thought of as a classic pop-song theme,
the poem charts the lifespan of a summer romance between
two young people falling in love for the first time, one of
those relationships that begins in June in the park and ends in
September in downpour.

THE GREAT WAR – AN ELEGY (2014)[*]

The poems in this publication formed part of a one-hour
documentary commissioned by the BBC, broadcast on BBC
Two, to coincide with the centenary of WWI. Over seven
hundred thousand British service personnel are estimated to
have lost their lives during that conflict, and the film followed
seven lesser-known or untold stories, notionally one story and
an accompanying poem for every hundred thousand dead. Com-
memoration was the film's central theme; as well as writing an
elegy, I wanted to consider how the fallen might be remembered
for the next one hundred years, now that the war is lost to living
memory. Through the work of Wilfred Owen, Siegfried Sassoon,
Robert Graves, Ivor Gurney and others, poetry and 'the Great
War' have become inextricably bound, so poetry felt like an
entirely appropriate, even natural mode of expression for telling
stories in the film, and exploring ideas, and paying respect.

---

[*] Introduction and notes from *Considering the Poppy*, privately published by
Andrew Moorhouse, Rochdale, 2014, with wood engravings by Chris Daunt.

I'd like to thank the BBC for providing the opportunity and means that allowed me to properly engage with this subject and for their confidence and trust through what was a long and logistically complex project. I'm particularly grateful to director Zoe Silver for her determination, thoughtfulness and creativity during the many months of filming and writing.

Sea Sketch

Edith Appleton was a trained nurse who kept a diary all the way through the war, recording the horrific injuries and agonising deaths of soldiers fighting in France. She nursed casualties from several battlefronts, including the Somme offensive, and wrote tenderly and compassionately about her patients. For many, hers was the last face they would see before passing away, and the last voice they would hear. While stationed in Normandy she visited the coast on days off, and made pencil sketches of the sea and the beach. Those drawings and their accompanying commentaries provide a relieving counterpoint to the graphic descriptions of life on the operating table and in the makeshift hospitals. The poem was read to camera by her great nephew, Dick Robinson, on the shingle beach at Étretat, a location made famous by Monet's paintings of the cliffs, and Edie's favourite place to swim and look out over the water.

Remains

Arthur Heath was a classicist, a fellow of New College, Oxford, and a brilliant young thinker and writer, engaged with ideas of political equality and social justice. On the eve of being called away to war he found solace and consolation in art, and continued to write inspiring, upbeat letters from the Western Front. During his time in military service he seemed to acknowledge death almost as an inevitability, and was killed in action on his twenty-eighth birthday. This poem turns its attention to the lost generation, that great swathe of the population whose potential was never realised and whose bones are still breaking surface in the fields of Belgium and France.

Considering the Poppy

The poppy is a 'ruderal', an opportunist species which takes advantage of fresh, raw soil and disturbed ground, which is why it flourished among the muddy trenches and blast-craters of the battlefields. As well as letters and documents, the archive of the Imperial War Museum, London, houses all kind of war-time paraphernalia, including a pressed poppy, picked for his wife in Devon by a soldier called Joseph Shaddick. The flower might have been a token of love, or recognised as a moment of colour and vibrancy among so much darkness and death, though no one at that time could have anticipated its role as an icon of remembrance. Leeched of its pigments and painfully brittle, Joseph Shaddick's hundred-year-old poppy looks like a butterfly fossil, or a drawing of a cross-section of the heart. It looks like an archetype.

Lazarus

Lieutenant James Bennett was one of twenty-nine men who escaped from 'escape-proof' Holzminden prison camp in Germany, and one of ten who made it home to Britain. Using spoons, knives and cups, inmates dug a tunnel sixty yards long from under the stone steps of the main block to a crop field on the other side of the fence. Holzminden is still in use as a German Army barracks, though not many people in the quiet town have heard of the escape or want to be reminded of the camp and its notoriously cruel commandant. James Bennett was only twenty-six at the time, and alerted his family to his arrival back in England with a telegram saying, 'Home this afternoon. Jim.' The poem was read by his daughter, Laurie Vaughan.

In Avondale

Amy Beechey lived on Avondale Street in Lincoln. Of her eight sons who went to war, five were killed: Harold, Barnard, Frank, Charles, Leonard. Their letters and postcards to their mother, from as far away as Gallipoli and Egypt, are held in the Lincolnshire Archives, many of them cheery and full of adventure. But the boxes contain more sombre and upsetting correspondence, standard forms filled in and signed by military administrators, beginning with the phrase, 'Dear Madam, it is my painful duty to inform you . . .' After the first such letter Amy would have recognised their shape and colour as they dropped through the letterbox; their meaning wasn't in doubt – it was a question of which name would be in the envelope, which son wouldn't be coming home.

The Thankful

Helperthorpe in the Yorkshire Wolds has no war memorial. It's one of just a handful of communities in Britain known as 'thankful villages', where all those who went off to the war came home. Inside the porch of St Peter's Church there's a roll of honour, 'in thankful memory of the safe return of all the men', and the first name on that list is Arthur Brown. Arthur was a Wagoner, driving a horse and cart through pastoral English farmland one minute, then next minute transporting munitions and supplies up the line and ferrying the wounded and dead back to base. Arthur Brown never travelled outside Britain again, and looked back at the war as a futile conflict. The poem was read by his grandson, Ted Atkinson, in his farmhouse a mile or so from the monument at Sledmere with its vivid depictions of the Wagoners at work in the fields of Yorkshire and the field of battle.

Memorial

The Clyne War Memorial stands at the side of the busy main road in the village of Brora on the east coast of Sutherland in the Scottish Highlands, and commemorates sixty-one soldiers from the area who lost their lives in WWI. It was paid for through voluntary contributions by local people. The memorial is also a functioning clock tower, maintained by the Keeper of the Clock, Jim Cunningham. For as long as it tells the right time and sends its chimes across the narrow river valley it means the structure has a useful purpose in the contemporary world, as well as standing as a reminder of the past. The memorial also remembers soldiers from WWII and from a more recent conflict in the Middle East. The blank spaces around the base of the tower seem to imply there will be more wars to come, more dead, more names to cut from the stone.

In Praise of Air (2014)

'The world's first catalytic poem' was written for the University of Sheffield in a project coordinated by Professor Joanna Gavins. Twenty metres high, ten metres wide, and suspended on the outside wall of the Alfred Denny Building on Western Bank, the poem is printed on an 'air-cleaning' catalytic surface developed by Professor Tony Ryan, designed to absorb nitric oxide from the atmosphere. After removing an estimated two tonnes of air pollution the poem was eventually taken down and cut into small sections, which were then framed and auctioned off to raise money for the British Lung Foundation.

IN A NUTSHELL (2014)

Three poems written for the BBC Radio 4 documentary *In a Nutshell*, produced and directed by Sue Roberts. 'Frances Glessner Lee revolutionised the study of crime investigation, founding the first centre for the study of forensic pathology at Harvard University. With a carpenter, Glessner Lee built a series of dolls' houses in the 1940s in which she constructed meticulous replica crime scenes to teach detectives their craft. These are still used in training new detectives today. Poet Simon Armitage travels to the Medical Examiner's office in Baltimore to investigate them, and their maker – regarded as the mother of modern CSI.' I became interested in the dioramas after reading

The Nutshell Studies of Unexplained Death by writer and photographer Corinne May Botz (The Monacelli Press, 2004) who was interviewed in the programme.

THE HENRY MOORE POEMS (2015)

Commissioned by Yorkshire Sculpture Park in connection with the *Henry Moore: Back to a Land* exhibition (2015) and first published in their book of the same name alongside images of the corresponding artworks. My preface to the poems read as follows:

'Until this exhibition I knew Henry Moore's work only by his larger pieces, those large bronzes often sited in public places, several of which are located within the grounds of Yorkshire Sculpture Park. It was a revelation and an adventure to discover more intimate, intricate and smaller scale work, both sculptures and drawings, and a rare privilege to be present during their unpacking and installation. In the funereal light of the Underground Gallery I felt to be witnessing a mass exhumation, followed by individual acts of resurrection as human shapes were lovingly unwrapped, raised and reintroduced to the world.

I chose to write about the five pieces and one photograph which made an immediate call on my attention and imagination, then sat in front of them and jotted down pages of words and phrases, much as a visual artist might make a few preparatory sketches. During those hours I recognised that a kind of daisy chain of reflection and refraction was taking place; Moore's art poeticises the physical world, and in turn I was recasting it through language and text.

As someone who has worked closely with Homer's *Odyssey* on several occasions I couldn't resist Moore's drawing of Odysseus in the cave, or resist seeing Moore himself as an Odyssean figure in Lee Miller's photograph of him in Holborn tube station during the Blitz. Consequently, and being mindful of Moore's preoccupation with geology, his background in the Yorkshire coalfields and his drawings of mines and miners, many of the poems developed subterranean themes. I also found myself engaging with the sexual politics of the work: what does it mean when a male sculptor says 'this is a woman', and what power dynamic or erotic charge takes place between the maker and his subject? The same question might be asked of the poet, standing in front of such nude female forms, describing their sensual beauty and putting words in their mouths.'

Artworks to which the poems refer:
Mother and Child (sculpture, Henry Moore, 1932)
Odysseus in the Cave of the Naiads (drawing, Henry Moore, 1944)
Women Winding Wool (drawing, Henry Moore, 1948)
Large Reclining Figure (sculpture, Henry Moore, 1984)
Henry Moore, Holborn Underground Station, London, England (photograph, Lee Miller, 1943)
Woman (sculpture, Henry Moore, 1957–58)

On the Existing State of Things (2015)

A version of a passage from Book VI of Virgil's *Aeneid*. In November 2015 the Bodleian Libraries, Oxford, acquired its twelve millionth printed book, a lost then found 'poetical essay' by 'a Gentleman of the University of Oxford' who was in fact the student Percy Bysshe Shelley. This poem was commissioned to mark the occasion, and was read at a launch event at the Weston Library, along with the following introductory remarks:

'The irony will have escaped no one. Just over two hundred years ago Percy Bysshe Shelley was ejected from this university on account of a controversial publication. Today he is welcomed back by the university through the acquisition of a controversial publication from the same period of his life. It's interesting to think of the smirk on the boyish face of the so-called ineffectual angel as he hovers above us, absent star of his own reunion.

By most accounts, Shelley was impetuous, antagonistic, really irritating at times, I imagine, character traits which are transmuted to passionate, determined and uncompromising by virtue of any good thesaurus. Freedom, independence and equality were his subjects, at a time when those concepts were thought by many to be a privilege rather than a right, and it's hard to identify a contemporary poet who addresses his or her concerns in such a forthright and challenging and convincing manner. Tony Harrison, perhaps; I struggled to come up with other names, in an age when subtlety and even a form of slyness dominates. Shelley is a poet who tells rather than shows. He doesn't so much throw down the gauntlet as slap us in the face with it, daring us to write with the courage of our convictions, even to *have* convictions in fact, and to identify our enemies and to address them head on.

Feeling that slap in the face, I wanted to respond by writing a poem – not exactly a dash to the barricades, I accept, but the only form of response I know, and to write a poem by the only method I know, which is to follow the ricochets and glances of coincidence and association and to let one idea lead to another. So when Shelley's unearthed poem rhymes 'war's dread roar' with 'blood-stain'd shore' I couldn't help but think of the plight of those hundreds of thousands of people currently trying to cross Shelley's beloved Mediterranean from one life to another. Those lines took me straight to Virgil's *Aeneid*, which I'm sure must have been in Shelley's mind as well, since echoes and cadences of Virgil rise and fall all the way through the Romantic poet's work, not least in the unfinished *The Triumph of Life* with its image of millions of lives as leaves in the breeze and birds in the sky, a handwritten copy of which is housed in this library. All those coincidences came into play, as did Shelley's own death in the same waters, and the notion that if Shelley had been alive and impetuous and passionate in our own age, this would have been his subject.'

POEMS IN THE AIR (2016)*

These six poems were commissioned by Northumberland National Park Authority, and came together under the title *Poems in the Air*. I'd been invited to write place-specific poetry for different locations in the Park, an area of over a thousand square kilometres made up of hill ranges, exposed moorland, wooded river valleys, forests, reservoirs, distant farms and picture-postcard towns, plus hundreds of sites of archaeological significance. Northumberland includes some of the most remote and underpopulated countryside in Britain, and I didn't want any physicalisation of the poems to disturb a geography whose emptiness and sparse beauty is part of its attraction and essential to its character. So they were presented as recordings only, in my voice, to be released by satellite technology within a five-yard radius of a specific map reference and delivered to mobile phones or other such portable listening devices. Poetry readings, of sorts, and in the very places where the poems are set, spread across an ancient, mystical and liminal border region.

A form of literary treasure hunting or geocaching, as well as encouraging people into the great outdoors and luring them towards some of the far-flung corners of the Park, the project was designed to offer an intimate experience, a non-intrusive but immersive coming together of landscape and language, between outer and inner worlds. Most poems exist as text; the 'ghost verses' of *Poems in the Air* were conceived as invisible entities, made only of digital coding, electromagnetic energy and breath, of which these published and illustrated versions are visible echoes and material afterthoughts.

---

* Introduction from *Exit The Known World*, privately published by Andrew Moorhouse, Rochdale, in 2018, with accompanying wood engravings by Hilary Paynter.

Map references:

'The Wishing Hole': NT 9277 0254
'November, 1962': NT 9671 1269
'Holywell Cottage and Black Pool': NY 8025 7694
'Hey Presto': NY 7901 8624
'A Proposal': NZ 0293 9838
'Homesteads': NT 9909 2394

Di-Di-Dah-Dah-Di-Dit (2016)

Commissioned for the four hundredth anniversary of Shakespeare's death and published in *On Shakespeare's Sonnets – A Poets' Celebration* (The Arden Shakespeare in association with the Royal Society of Literature, ed. Hannah Crawforth and Elizabeth Scott-Baumann, 2016). The poem was accompanied by the following note:

'At school, Shakespeare's sonnets were usually presented as riddles rather than poems, things that had to be solved before they could be understood or enjoyed. For some they continue to be cryptograms, coded messages embedded with information about the poet's life, his religion, his authorship of the work and of course his sexuality, of which Sonnet XX is often said to be the most revealing. I have pricked out my own coded sonnet in response.'

Hence (2016)

Commissioned by Winchester Poetry Festival. 'The Artist undertakes to write and deliver a new poem no longer than twenty-four lines in response to Antony Gormley's *Sound II* sculpture in Winchester Cathedral.' The poem was published in the Festival programme and also on postcards with accompanying artwork.

MANSIONS IN THE SKY – THE RISE AND FALL OF
BRANWELL BRONTË (2017)

This suite of poems was written as part of a year-long creative
partnership with the Brontë Parsonage Museum. My Foreword
and Introduction, taken from the exhibition guidebook, sets out
the background to the project and explains my responses, and
is followed by catalogue entries detailing the items of Branwell
memorabilia on which the poems were based and alongside
which they were displayed.

*

'When the Brontë Parsonage Museum asked me to curate
an exhibition and a series of events around Branwell Brontë's
bicentenary I knew straightaway that I wanted to do it, but had no
idea how. In what way is it possible to celebrate someone whose
achievements are insignificant compared to the accomplishments
of his siblings, and whose life was ultimately a source of
humiliation, distress and grief to his family? At first I wondered
if the infamous 'black sheep' version of Branwell was there to
be reappraised. Or whether, behind the bad-boy caricature,
there was a neglected and misunderstood genius waiting to be
revealed. There wasn't, but what I began to appreciate in reading
and researching Branwell was a young man of fierce ambition
and hyperactive creativity, someone whose imagination and
personality had an incalculable effect on the writings of his
sisters and the day-to-day mood in the house they all shared,
and someone for whom I ultimately felt an enormous amount
of sympathy. W. H. Auden once famously remarked that it was
every poet's hope to be 'like some valley cheese: local, but prized
elsewhere', and as a poet of the same hills and moors as Branwell
I recognised his desire to be acknowledged and affirmed by the
wider world.

The *Mansions in the Sky* exhibition is presented in two parts.
Downstairs in the Bonnell Room at the Parsonage I have selected

for display objects and items belonging to or associated with Branwell, from some of his writings and drawings to his rather weird masonic apron, and have responded to each of them with a poem of my own. Some of the poems are deliberately anachronistic, mentioning Paul Pogba, for example, the world's most expensive footballer (at the time of writing), and listing modern-day paraphernalia among the contents of Branwell's wallet. Another of the poems references the band The Smiths, because it occurred to me that if anyone would have pinned a picture of Morrissey on his wall it would have been Branwell, though perhaps stolen from Emily's room. I suppose the intention here is to consider how we might relate to a Branwell-like character in our own day and age, or to place the historical Branwell in equivalent contemporary situations.

Think of the Bonnell Room as the exterior world. Upstairs, and with the expert help of the production team from the BBC film *To Walk Invisible*, the room that Branwell worked and slept in has been recreated (and in the very room he worked and slept in). Think of this as the interior world; my aim is to make visitors entering that room feel as if they have walked into Branwell's head, a chaotic and frenzied place, especially towards the end of his life.

But my starting point for *Mansions in the Sky* was a letter, and a poem containing that phrase, sent to William Wordsworth by Branwell in January 1837 when he was nineteen years old. The letter is a little pretentious, a little precocious and not a little presumptuous, and like the voice in the poem it's also daring, wistful, even desperate at times, so to me perfectly encapsulates Branwell's biography as it would unfold, or perhaps I should say unravel. The letter is displayed in the exhibition (Wordsworth didn't reply but at least he didn't throw it on the fire), and my poem in reply imagines Branwell picturing Wordsworth reading his astounding work of ground-breaking brilliance, before reality sets in.

If one word characterises Branwell's life then I think that word is disappointment. He was a disappointment to others, but more painfully to himself. Just as Charlotte's star was rising,

Branwell's burnt-out hope was travelling just as quickly in the opposite direction, and after dreaming of heaven, and building his mansions in the sky, planet earth was never really going to be good enough. His was a pitiful end; great sorrows had preceded it and more would follow soon afterwards, all part of a most incredible true story worthy of the wildest fiction.'*

Letter to Wordsworth ('William, It was Really Nothing')

Branwell Brontë
10 January 1837
Wordsworth Trust

A letter from Branwell Brontë to William Wordsworth, enclosing a poetry manuscript titled 'The Struggles of Flesh with Spirit'.

> '... Read it sir and as you would hold a light to one in utter darkness as you value your own kind heartedness return me an answer if but one word telling me whether I should write on or write no more'.

Wordsworth, 'disgusted with the letter' according to poet Robert Southey, did not reply.

Masonic apron ('Initiation')

c.1836/7
Private owner

Masonic apron reputedly decorated by Branwell Brontë for Three Graces Lodge, the Haworth freemasons, of which he was made a member on 29 February 1836 and later became secretary. Watercolour on white canvas decorated with Masonic symbols.

---

* Thanks are due to Ann Dinsdale, Principal Curator, Brontë Society & Brontë Parsonage Museum, for her part in the preparation of the notes to these poems.

Branwell's wallet ('Wallet')

H134

A folding wallet made of (now faded) red leather and cardboard.

Luddenden Foot notebook ('Lost and Found')

c.1841–1842
BS127

Pocket book owned by Branwell during his period of employment at Luddenden Foot, working on the Leeds and Manchester Railway. Branwell uses the notebook to record his professional tasks as well as sketches, drawings, poetry and notes. He was dismissed from this employment in March 1842.

Self portrait ('Self Portrait')

Branwell Brontë
c.1840
Bonnell 18

A caricature self portrait by Branwell, depicting in side profile his spectacles, high collar and prominent nose.

The Monthly Intelligencer ('The Smallprint')

1833
BS117

Manuscript newspaper created by Branwell Brontë, titled *The Monthly Intelligencer: a few words to the Chief Genii*. The manuscript was produced in detail to replicate an authentic newspaper.

Little Henry ('Little Henry')

1810
B32

The History and Adventures of Little Henry was published in 1810; this paperback book contains seven cut-out card figures to accompany the story. It was given to the Brontë siblings during their childhood.

The Politics of Verdopolis ('Verdopolis')

Branwell Brontë
15 November 1833
Bonnell 141.7

Ink on paper sketch depicting a tall building, with nearby bridge across a river. The building features on one of the manuscript pages of *The Politics of Verdopolis: a tale by Captain John Flower MP*, which forms part of the Glasstown series of juvenilia. The way in which the text wraps around the drawing is typical of Branwell's graphic style.

Gos Hawk ('The Gos Hawk')

Branwell Brontë
1833
B9

Watercolour and pencil painting of a Goshawk, copied from Thomas Bewick's *A History of British Birds*.

A Parody ('The End')

Branwell Brontë
*c.*22 July 1848
B28

A drawing in the style of a cartoon, depicting Branwell in bed, summoned by Death. This is the last known drawing by Branwell who died on 24 September 1848, and gives an insight into the 'agony of mind' experienced during his last few months.

A Twofold (2017)

Published in *Christmas Crackers, Ten Poems to Surprise and Delight* (Candlestick Press, 2017).

FLIT (2018)

A book-length collection with accompanying photographs by the author (ably assisted by Sarah Coulson, for which, many thanks). The forty poems were the culmination of a writer-residency to mark the fortieth anniversary of Yorkshire Sculpture Park in 2017, and were published by YSP the following year.

The Handshake (2018)

Commissioned by Carol Ann Duffy for the anthology *Armistice* (Faber & Faber, 2018).

The Brink (2019)

The poetic script for a film commissioned by Sky Arts for their Art 50 project, produced by Jim Poyser and directed by Jason Wingard. The brief was encouragingly open: a shortish film-poem about Britain's relationship with Europe, and although transmission was scheduled to coincide with Britain's official withdrawal from the EU in March 2019, Brexit was never specified as the subject (unless I misread the contract, deliberately or otherwise). The poem follows a train journey to Britain's south-east coast, looking out over the English Channel towards 'the Continent', considering matters of proximity and distance.